DYING, AS A FRANCISCAN:

APPROACHING OUR TRANSITUS TO ETERNAL LIFE
ACCOMPANYING OTHERS ON THE WAY TO THEIRS

Volume 15   *2011*

Spirit and Life: Essays on Contemporary Franciscanism serves as a vehicle for the publication of papers presented at various conferences, symposia, and/or workshops that seek to bring the Franciscan tradition into creative dialogue with contemporary theology, philosophy, and history.

During the fiftieth anniversary year of The Franciscan Institute (1991), the publication of this series was a refounding of an earlier Franciscan Institute Series entitled *Spirit and Life*, established in 1948 by the Reverend Philotheus Boehner, O.F.M., one of the co-founders and first director of The Franciscan Institute.

The Franciscan Institute is deeply grateful to the May Bonfils Trust Fund and the Holy Name Province for their assistance with the Forum.

SPIRIT AND LIFE

ESSAYS ON CONTEMPORARY FRANCISCANISM

VOLUME 15   2011

DYING, AS A FRANCISCAN:

APPROACHING OUR TRANSITUS TO ETERNAL LIFE
ACCOMPANYING OTHERS ON THE WAY TO THEIRS

Series Editor:
Michael F. Cusato, O.F.M.

Volume Editor:
Daria Mitchell, O.S.F.

CONTENTS

Our Contributors

Michael F. Cusato, O.F.M., is Dean of The School of Franciscan Studies and Director of The Franciscan Institute, St. Bonaventure University, St. Bonaventure, NY. A noted contemporary Franciscan historian, he has published a collection of his studies titled *The Early Franciscan Movement (1205-1239): History, Sources, and Hermeneutics.*

Thomas Nairn, O.F.M., is the Senior Director of Ethics at the Catholic Health Association, U.S.A. Prior to this appointment, he served as the Erica and Harry John Family Professor of Catholic Ethics at Catholic Theological Union. He holds a Ph.D., from the University of Chicago Divinity School. He has lectured or given workshops in the U.S., Australia, Great Britain, Ireland, Japan, Kenya, Papua New Guinea, Singapore, South Africa, Trinidad, and Zimbabwe.

Mary Petrosky, F.M.M., is a member of the Franciscan Missionaries of Mary. She presently ministers as a Spiritual Director at the Franciscan Center for Spirituality and Spiritual Direction at St. Francis of Assisi Church in Manhattan.

Kathleen McCarron, O.S.F., is a Sister of St. Francis of Philadelphia. She is a licensed social worker and has worked with religious congregations companioning sisters through life transitions. Kate served as a General Council member from 2002-2008, and is currently a counselor in the community retirement facility.

Daniel Sulmasy, O.F.M., M.D., Ph.D., is a Franciscan Friar, the Kilbride-Clinton Professor of Medicine and Ethics in the Department of Medicine and Divinity School at the University of Chicago, where he serves as Associate Director of the MacLean Center for Clinical Medical Ethics. He has previously held faculty positions at New York Medical College and at Georgetown Univeristy. He received his A.B. and M.D. degrees from Cornell University and completed his residency, chief residency and post-doctoral fellowship in General Internal Medicine at the Johns Hopkins Hospital.

DYING, AS A FRANCISCAN

Many of us within the Franciscan Family of the twenty-first century – friars, sisters, seculars and all those associated in any way with the Poverello of Assisi – find ourselves surrounded by those within our own communities and families who are in need of accompaniment and companionship as they walk the road toward the fullness of life. And each one of us, one day, will walk the same path ourselves.

Numerous poignant artistic depictions in the famous Giotto frescoes show us the dying Francis and Clare being cared for and mourned by brothers and sisters gathered around them during the final days of their lives. These beloved friends of our founders journeyed with them, preparing them for that great *transitus* which would take each of them from this life through death into eternal life.

Is there a particularly Franciscan manner of approaching our own passage to the Lord and of helping others to do the same? Are there particular elements within the Franciscan tradition – stories, symbols, rituals, and so forth – on which we can all draw to help us and others whom we accompany in this ultimate pilgrimage of the human journey? There are indeed! On June 17-20, 2010, the Ninth National Franciscan Forum explored both aspects of this journey through a series of talks and discussions led by a group of distinguished presenters including: Michael F. Cusato, O.F.M.; Thomas Nairn, O.F.M.; Mary Petrosky, F.M.M.; Daniel Sulmasy, O.F.M.; Thomas Lynch; Kathleen McCarron, O.S.F. Held on the scenic campus of Regis University in Denver, Colorado, the Forum allowed presenters and participants the opportunity to delve deeply into their shared experience of sharing with, ministering to, and personally preparing for the *transitus* from earthly to eternal life.

In this volume you can experience, in a vicarious manner, elements of the journey our presenters and participants took in their investigation of death and dying with a specifically Franciscan interpretation. Beginning with the reflection given by Michael Cusato during the opening prayer service –an adapted *transitus* service for Francis and Clare of Assisi – we look at the challenges we face in acknowledging an increasing awareness of our fragility, of our need for the companionship of and our responsibility to be companions to our brothers and sisters on that same journey with us, and finally accepting the grace to make that final act of surrender to our Good God.

Thomas Nairn then opens up the early *legendae* and the writings of St. Bonaventure to begin a dialogue about what it meant to Francis and Clare to be lovingly embraced by Sister Death. Francis and Clare died surrounded by those who loved them and whom they loved. Similarly, members of the Franciscan family who are facing serious illness and death need to know that their sisters and brothers are around them.

Mary Petrosky takes the discussion from the aspects of the process of dying – physically, emotionally, and intellectually – which can be considered universal to a recognition that the experience of dying is also singularly individual. Much of the individuality of the experience can be shaped, nurtured and deeply affected by one's spirituality. In the end Francis teaches us much about Death, but also much about Life. "Francis knew how to die because Francis knew how to live."

Continuing with the connection between how Francis lived and how he died, Mary then draws attention to the challenges we face today in accepting the diminishment which is happening in our bodies, our minds, and our spirits, which calls us to enter into a new phase of our lives. This transition most often means less physical activity with the gradual (if not sudden) withdrawal from the ministries which gave us life. How do we help our brothers and sisters to accept their new ministry of aging?

Kate McCarron expands the discussion, considering three themes: mindfulness, wisdom and transparency. Mindfulness leads to integrity and authenticity. Wisdom is the second characteristic achieved through successful transitioning and leads to self-awareness. Finally, in transparency, we realize that God continues to call us to life until our last breath. "The center of our Franciscan call is a life of conversion of heart, and the real heart of the matter is our final conversion, our final turn from life as we know it, to the fullness of life, eternal life."

Kate next looks at how caregivers must reach out to those who are moving through the stages of the final transition. It is important, in caring for our own, to help them identify what is needed now, to help the ongoing transformative conversions that are taking place in their lives until they take their last breath. There is a delicate balance here that we must maintain, a stepping back and allowing the other to be transformed; allowing them to be as involved as they want to be.

Daniel Sulmasy then talked about ethical issues when caring for people at the end of life within the Catholic tradition. Suffering is an experience that makes explicit the inherent tension between our intrinsic dignity and our finitude. Illness is a fact of life but it is also a mystery. The goals of medicine are to minister to this mystery of the human between our dignity, our God and our finitude: to cure sometimes, to relieve often and to comfort always.

Thomas Nairn directs the discussion to end-of-life care, stating that it cannot be limited to the physical but should also "embrace the physical, psychological, social, and spiritual dimensions of the human person." So spiritual care during sickness and especially at the end of life can help a brother or sister cope with feelings of powerlessness in suffering and can make it easier for the person to see meaning, and even redemption, in suffering.

Looking at issues involved following death, Daniel Sulmasy discusses death certificates, autopsies and other legal realities before leading us back to the awareness that the dead are with us even though in a different manner. We may never have noticed but they have become necessary parts of who we are, of what constitutes us now as persons. The people who have loved us deeply, even though they have died, have fallen into the mystery of God who is the love beyond all love and beyond all horizon and circumscribers. This God, as Bonaventure once wrote, is the one whose center is everywhere and whose circumference is nowhere. The dead are with us in that holy love.

In the homily of the liturgy for the 12th Sunday of the Year, Michael Cusato leads us through the Gospel story of Peter's answer when Christ asks, "But you, who do you say I am?" Peter's answer names Jesus the Christ. But the name or title *Christos* means more than simply "You are God's *App*ointed!" To be the "*An*ointed of God" means that you are God's "chrism"; you are God's healing balm for all of us who are his people. And if Christ's role is to be a healing presence among us, so, too, is it the same role for those of us who bear the name of "Christian": we are to be, for each other, a "chrismatic" people: healing balm for one another, binding up the wounds inflicted by life during this sacred journey.

At the conclusion of the Ninth National Franciscan Forum, the presentations were gathered into this volume for your reference and reflection. It is our hope that continued reflection on our *transitus* from this life to life within the eternal embrace of our God will make us more

authentic witnesses to that reality experienced by Francis, Clare and all our brothers and sisters who welcomed Sister Death as a dear companion for the journey to eternal life.

The presentations by Thomas Lynch were difficult to render in print form but are available with the complete proceedings of the Ninth National Franciscan Forum on five DVDs from www. ruahmedia.org

"Dying, as a Franciscan"
Transitus Homily

Michael F. Cusato, O.F.M.

The men and women of the Middle Ages had a word, a phrase, to describe us: each one of us was a *homo viator* – a human person on the road, on a journey (from one place to another). The story we have heard this evening – the two stories intertwined with each other into one – is the story of such a journey. And we have been privileged to catch a glimpse of that journey as it nears its endpoint, during the last weeks and days of the lives of Francis and Clare. That journey speaks to us not just because we are all, in some way, Franciscans; but because we are all human beings on a shared journey of life.

Many, if not most, of us have heard these readings before. Heard, however, in the context of our gathering this weekend, perhaps fresh details might have leapt up into your imagination. Three themes in particular impressed themselves upon me; I've crystallized them into three phrases.

1. The first theme is the *disheartening discovery of our own fragility*. The deaths of Francis and Clare were both preceded by prolonged periods of illness and decline. As such, they presage or portend what will be for many of us – though not all of us – our own journeys into that good night. For, at the end of the day, we are all rather fragile persons: we get sick, we age; our bodies and our minds begin to break down, to fail us, to fool us, to embarrass us. Sometimes the mind goes before the body; and sometimes it's the other way around; and there's no way of telling which will come first. We wound; we bruise; we bleed;

we become overwhelmed, depressed and withdrawn. We scale
the heights of strength, agility and acumen; but then start to
fade and stumble in decline. This is a grace that is unwelcome;
but it allows us to discover a hitherto unacknowledged aspect
of our creaturehood as our journey begins to bend back toward
God while we are yet here.

2.   And then, in the midst of this dismaying discovery of our fra-
     gility, we are given a second grace: *the presence and the care of
     our brothers and sisters*. Virtually in every scene this evening,
     our sister Clare and our brother Francis were surrounded and
     comforted by their brothers and sisters – and sometimes even
     both: men and women, companions on the common journey
     of life and faith, who gathered around, sometimes in silence,
     sometimes in prayer, sometimes in song, as companionable,
     faith-filled presences in our time of need, in our time of fear,
     in our time of contrition, as we prepare for the moment of our
     passage. Just as each one of us has been accompanied by oth-
     ers on *our* journey of faith from our earliest years in the com-
     munity, so now it is one of the greatest gifts *we* can give to one
     another to accompany each other at this sacred time of life.
     Sometimes, we gather because we have been close companions;
     sometimes, because we simply share the bond of a common vo-
     cation; and sometimes, too, we who have been estranged from
     or have estranged the other gather in vigil, willing to put aside
     the hurts of the past in the service of a higher calling: fraternal
     or sororal accompaniment.

3.   And not long thereafter, a third and final grace is given: the
     grace of a *faith-propelled act of surrender*. Both Francis and Clare
     died as they had lived: as persons of real and living faith. Be-
     yond reporting on their illnesses and the experience of their
     physical decline, our hagiographers do not tell us if they, like
     so many of us, experience inner doubts and fears at the mo-
     ment of passage. What we do know is this: that they made of
     their final moments a profound act of surrender, asking the
     Lord, in the words of the Psalm, to lead them forward into
     the loving hands of God. We, too, if given this opportunity,

can transform our lives into a final moment of prayer: make of our lives an act of *faith-propelled prayer*: placing in the hands of the Lord the pain of our decline, the sinfulness that has been unacknowledged and yet un-atoned, indeed the totality of our whole lives, trusting that the Lord will accept the simple offer of our complex gift as our final act of love and fidelity.

Thus, this is a privileged time of grace. Because we share the human condition, we all walk the same journey. Because we share a life in common, with sisters, brothers and associates at our sides, we do not walk this journey alone. And because we share a life of faith, the journey we walk is never aimless, never a dead-end. It is, rather, always a *transitus*: a journey from here to there, from our human life together to our life with God forever, when the beating of our hearts will stop only to be taken up, lovingly and assuredly, into the beating heart of God.

"Fixed with Christ to the Cross": Dying in the Franciscan Tradition

Thomas A. Nairn, O.F.M.

Members of the Franciscan family follow "the footprints of our Lord Jesus Christ" (ER 1) by following the examples of Francis and Clare. Since *example* was a critical dimension in the lives of both of these saints, the early Franciscan family considered *stories* to be important. It is no accident that in the years after their deaths, stories and *legendae* regarding both saints flourished. Today, their followers still gather annually to commemorate their deaths by re-telling their story and sharing in their *Transitus*. We relate again the details of their passing from this life to the next. How different from our contemporary images of sickness and dying do their stories seem! Yet even the apparent foreignness of these stories can help us understand what it means to die as a Franciscan.

This essay will investigate how the Franciscan tradition has understood death and dying. It will first look at the experience of Francis and Clare as described in the early *legendae* in order to try to find some insight into their understanding of what it means to be lovingly embraced by Sister Death. It will then look to the writings of St. Bonaventure to discover how the lives and deaths of Francis and Clare affected the Franciscan theological tradition. The essay will end with a brief look at the writings of St. Bernardine of Siena to raise a similar question regarding how the Franciscan spiritual tradition wrestled with death and dying.[1]

---

[1] This paper brings together elements found in two earlier articles: Thomas Nairn, "The Last Illness of Francis," *The Cord* 47.5 (1997): 206-12, and "Is Death a

The Examples of Francis and Clare

St. Bonaventure describes that, having received the gift of the stigmata, St. Francis spent the last two years of his life dealing with chronic illness. He explains: "Francis now hung, body and soul, upon the Cross with Christ" (LMj 14:1). St. Clare spent the last twenty-eight of her sixty years of life with a chronic sickness, much of that time bedridden.[2] We often tend to romanticize the lives of these saints, but we also need to recall that they both became debilitated by chronic (and eventually terminal) illnesses. Their own stories include those values that can help us learn what it means to die as a Franciscan.

Since stories are so important for the Franciscan family, it is wise to begin this investigation with a series of stories, the first of which comes from the *Assisi Compilation* and describes a conversation that St. Francis had with his own physician, a doctor named "Good John":

> During those days a doctor from the city of Arezzo, named Good John, who was known and familiar to blessed Francis, came to visit him.... Blessed Francis asked about his sickness, saying: "How does my illness of dropsy seem to you, Brother John?" ... The doctor said to him: "Brother, by the grace of God, it will be well with you." For the doctor did not want to tell him that he would die in a little while. Again blessed Francis said to him: "Tell me the truth. How does it look to you? Do not be afraid; for, by the grace of God, I am not a coward who fears death. With the Lord's help, by his mercy and grace, I am so united and joined to my Lord that I am equally as happy to die as I am to live" (AC 100).

It is often said that "the more things change, the more things remain the same." One is able to see this sentiment in the above story. Notice that what the physician says is technically correct: *with God's*

Moral Problem for the Franciscan Intellectual Tradition?" in *Moral Action in a Complex World: Franciscan Perspectives*, ed. Daria Mitchell (St. Bonaventure, NY: Franciscan Institute Publications, 2008), 93-120.

[2] *Legend of St. Clare*, 39. *The Acts of the Process of Canonization of St. Clare of Assisi* states that her illness lasted twenty-nine years. See "Witness of Sr. Pacifica," 17. The above references can be found in *Clare of Assisi Early Documents: The Lady*, rev. ed. and trans. Regis J. Armstrong, O.F.M. Cap. (New York: New City Press, 2006), 313 and 149 respectively; hereafter cited as *CA:ED* followed by page.

grace, all will be well for St. Francis. At the same time the inference the doctor made was false: he knew that Francis would soon die. It sounds like he did not want his patient to lose hope. Not much has changed since Francis's talk with his doctor. Physicians today can also explain end-of-life situations in such a way as to give patients or their families false hope, thinking that hope can only be understood in terms of cure, even when such a cure is virtually impossible.

Responding to his doctor, St. Francis asked that he be told the truth. Almost eight centuries after the deaths of Francis and Clare, the issue of truth telling remains controversial. Even as others question what should or should not be told to a dying person, it seems that the followers of Francis and Clare need to be truthful, speaking the truth about the sickness of our sisters and brothers and even about our own sickness and dying. Such truthfulness demands courage both on the part of those who speak and on the part of those who are willing to listen. Following the example of Francis, we see, however, that speaking the truth never means that we simply give up on the patient. Illness, suffering, and death threaten human wellbeing and dignity. It is proper to resist them to the extent that we are able. But, following the example of Francis, we do not *fear* sickness and dying. If we believe that the paschal mystery proclaims victory over death, we also believe with courage that it is precisely in our vulnerability that we encounter the crucified and risen Christ. Grave illness *can* be a time of grace. Our faith tells us that God is present even in the midst of illness, suffering, and death. Death can truly become a sister to us.

The story of Francis continues. Thomas of Celano explains how the brothers dealt with Francis's illness, describing it as a community of care:

> For nearly two years he endured these things with complete patience and humility, in all things giving thanks to God. But in order to be able to devote his attention to God more freely, he entrusted his own care to certain brothers, who with good reason were very dear to him.... These men, vigilantly, zealously, and eagerly protected the peace of mind of the blessed father, cared for him in his illness, and spared no pain or labor in offering themselves completely to the saint's service (1C 102).

Looking in a similar way to the sickness of Clare, we see that her sisters spoke of her love for others in terms of the care she showed her sisters. During the process of canonization, one of her sisters witnessed that Clare always "had compassion for the sick. While she was healthy, she served them and washed their feet and gave them water with her own hands. Sometimes she washed the mattresses of the sick."[3] To see the example with its full impact, one should not think of sickness and mattresses as one would see them in a contemporary medical center or even one's home. Rather, the sickness of the sisters at the time of Clare would have included oozing sores and other bodily fluids soiling the mattresses that Clare washed. Still another witness explained:

> One time when five sisters were sick in the monastery, Saint Clare made the sign of the cross with her own hand over them and all of them were immediately cured. Frequently when one of the sisters had some pain in either the head or another part of the body, the blessed mother cured her with the sign of the cross.[4]

The example of Francis and Clare offers an important counterpoint to the attitude often expressed in contemporary medicine. Many physicians today suppose that the purpose of medicine is to cure disease. This implies that it is only when cure is no longer possible that the doctor's focus may change to "caring" for the patient. In this understanding, however, caring is always something less than curing, a "second class" response to the disease, to be used only when the "real" curative attempts have failed.

Contrasted with this, the Catholic position has been that we always care. When patients are appropriately resisting the onslaught of disease, especially at the beginning of a disease, the caring thing to do is to help them fight the disease and try to cure them if this is possible. In this situation, cure and care are identical. However, in the late stages of a terminal disease, there does come a time when to continue aggressive treatment directed at curing the patient is no longer truly caring. In fact, it might in actuality harm the patient. At this time, one needs to ask: What *is* the caring thing to do?

---

[3] *Process of Canonization*, Witness 1, 12, *CA:ED* 147.
[4] *Process of Canonization*, Witness 1, 16, *CA:ED* 149.

In order for our sisters and brothers who are facing serious illness or death to accept it as a time of grace, the rest of the Franciscan family must exhibit a spirit that witnesses to faithfulness and care. If we expect our sick and dying brothers and sisters to speak the truth about their illness and death, then as a caring community we must be honest with *them*. If they are called to witness to a spirit of dependence, then we must be a community that is *dependable*. If they are to give an example of letting go and not clinging to the last remnant of life, then we must not abandon them in their suffering but rather *care* for them.

Becoming a community of faithfulness and care does not come automatically. Especially in our time, conflicts are inevitable. This may be especially true as we recognize ethnic, cultural, and even familial differences within the community. Because of our own particular backgrounds, we may not always understand the needs of a particular sick brother or sister. Nevertheless Franciscans are called to be that community of faithfulness that a sister or brother requires in her or his need.

The story of Francis moves towards its conclusion. St. Bonaventure describes the last days of the saint:

> In that grave illness that ended all suffering, he threw himself in fervor of spirit totally naked on the naked ground so that in that final hour, when the enemy could still rage, he might wrestle naked with the naked enemy. Lying like this on the ground, stripped of his sackcloth garment, he lifted up his face to heaven, in his accustomed way, and wholly intent upon that glory, he covered with his left hand the wound in his right side, so that no one would see it. And he said to his brothers, "I have done what is mine; may Christ teach you yours" (LMj 14:3).

Similarly, the *Legend of St. Clare* explains:

> For forty years she had run the course of the highest poverty, when, preceded by a number of illnesses, she was obviously approaching the prize of her exalted calling. Since the strength of her flesh had succumbed to the austerity of the penance of her early years, a harsh sickness took hold of her last years, so that she who had been enriched with the merits of good deeds

when well might be enriched with the merits of suffering when sick. For virtue is brought to perfection in sickness.... How her marvelous virtue had been perfected in her sickness will be hereafter told at length: because during her twenty-eight years of her prolonged sickness she did not murmur or utter a complaint, but holy comments and thanksgiving always came from her mouth.[5]

It then describes her death:

It was finally seen that she was laboring for many days in her last agony during which the faith of the neighboring regions and the devotion of the peoples increased.... But since the Lord was very near and, as it were, already at the door, she wished the priests and her spiritual brothers to stand by and read the Passion of the Lord and holy words.... Finally she turned to her weeping daughters to whom she recalled in a praising way the divine blessings while entrusting them with the poverty of the Lord.... She then spoke to herself: "Go without anxiety, for you have a good escort for your journey. Go, for he who created you has made you holy. And, always protecting you as a mother her child, he has loved you with a tender love."[6]

Francis and Clare died surrounded by those who loved them and whom they loved. Similarly, members of the Franciscan family who are facing serious illness and death need to know that their sisters and brothers are around them. When appropriately resisting the onslaughts of disease, they need to experience the encouragement of their sisters and brothers. As illness progresses, they should be able to depend on their communities to give physical and spiritual comfort. Finally, as disease enters into its last stages and death approaches, they should be confident in the presence of others and the reassurance that they will not be abandoned.

Those caring for a seriously ill or dying brother or sister may also need to ask whether their own expectations regarding another's suffering are appropriate. There might be times when a caregiver might

[5] *Legend of St. Clare*, 39, *CA:ED* 313.
[6] *Legend of St. Clare*, 45, *CA:ED* 316.

think that the sick person is over-reacting. There may be other times when a caregiver will want to make everything right and "fix" things even when the only appropriate response is merely to remain present and powerless with the brother or sister who is suffering. At other times the caregiver's own dis-ease with death may keep her or him from being truly present to the sick sister or brother. In all of this the words of Francis return to help guide us, "I have done what is mine; may Christ teach you yours."

Through this brief look at the lives of Francis and Clare, especially the end of their lives, we not only see the fact that death is a sister in the lives of the saints, but we are also given some practical guidance that is as true in the twenty-first century as it was in the thirteenth.

THE FRANCISCAN THEOLOGICAL TRADITION:
ST. BONAVENTURE

A profound reflection upon the life and example of Francis gave birth to the Franciscan intellectual tradition in theology and philosophy. Early Franciscan scholars in schools such as Paris and Oxford began to use the spiritual insights of the saint as the basis for an all-encompassing theological vision. This theological vision moves the discussion from the practical issues of how Franciscans can prepare for death and dying to the issue of what death itself means for Franciscans. In this section, I will briefly investigate the writings of St. Bonaventure (1221-1274), concentrating on two aspects of his thought that demonstrate two somewhat contradictory meanings of death: his theology of *transitus*, which recognizes death as a passing into glory, and his teaching regarding the resurrection of the body, which acknowledges death as a painful separation of soul and body.

Death as Transitus

Members of the Franciscan family are familiar with the term *transitus*. Most have taken part in the ritual that occurs during the evening of October 3 and commemorates the death of St. Francis, his "passing over" into glory. At home with this ceremony, we should not be surprised that St. Bonaventure often uses the term *transitus* when he is

discussing death. Actually, in his writings this term has a variety of related meanings. In an article analyzing the spiritual dimensions of the
term, André Ménard speaks of six different uses of the term *transitus* in
the writings of Bonaventure: contemplation (19 citations), the paschal
mystery (12 citations), death and dying (12 citations), renunciation (6
citations), the passing nature of creation (4 citations), and the opposi-
tion between the transitory and the unchanging (3 citations).[7]

Ménard argues that – central to Bonaventure's use of the term – the
very core of the Franciscan spiritual life is the passion and resurrection
of our Lord Jesus. He suggests that by using this term Bonaventure
"invites us to become more aware that everything takes place in order
that we might enter into the dynamism of the movement initiated by
Christ. The meaning of every human adventure is participation with
Christ and, in Christ, in the life offered us by God."[8] If this is true,
then for Bonaventure the *transitus* of death is best understood as the
transitus of one's passing from the transitory to the unchanging, from
this imperfect life into glory. In commenting on this *transitus*, Ménard
explains:

> It is simply the *transitus* we make through the *reductio integra*
> [complete return] that is our death. We return to the Father,
> the fontal principle of all that is; we enter the sanctuary of wis-
> dom where we discover "the reason of living things" and "the
> dwellings of the predestined." We enter into loving ecstasy,
> finding our delight in the contemplation of the one who gives
> himself to us in his humanity and his divinity. Our happiness
> is complete.[9]

This *transitus* demands our leaving what is passing and fully entering into that glory which is the Kingdom of God.

Ménard concludes that, according to Bonaventure, "created being cannot provide a rational foundation for our life. Revelation tells
us that our deepest desire can be realized only by sharing in the very
life of God."[10] True life awaits us in heaven, and it is death that serves

---

[7] André Ménard, O.F.M. Cap., "The Spirituality of *Transitus* in the Writings of St.
Bonaventure," *Greyfriars Review* 18.1 (2004): 24-25.

[8] Ménard, "The Spirituality of *Transitus* ...," 50-51.

[9] Ménard, "The Spirituality of *Transitus* ...," 44.

[10] Ménard, "The Spirituality of *Transitus* ...," 44.

as the entry point. While we are on earth we are merely pilgrims. He quotes from the *Major Life of St. Francis*, where Bonaventure described Francis as "passing from this world to the Father, passing through the desert of the word like pilgrims and strangers and like true Hebrews" (LMj, VII:9). Ménard explains:

> According to the etymologies of Jerome and Isidore of Seville, "Hebrew" means "one who is passing through" or "pilgrim." The brothers are the true Hebrews, the true descendents of Abraham in faith.... They too must cross a desert, the world, before arriving in the promised last, heaven. With Jesus they must pass from this world to the Father.[11]

Bonaventure's understanding of *transitus* acknowledges that death is triumph. It is the passing from earthly life to eternal life, from the transitory to the unchanging. This element of his theology understands death and dying as one's entrance into the glorious life of the Kingdom of Heaven to be spent eternally with God. For a Franciscan, dying and entering into glory is the goal of one's life.

The Resurrection of the Body

Bonaventure's use of the term *transitus* helps contemporary Franciscans understand the passing nature of earthly life and the glory of the life to come. Looking further into his eschatology, however, especially into his understanding of death as the separation of the soul from body, adds a different dimension to the question of the status of death for Bonaventure, one that is more ambiguous.

In his theological treatise called the *Breviloquium*, Bonaventure discusses the resurrection of the body after the final judgment. He states that the final blessedness "must be brought about in a way that respects the rectitude of justice, the restoration of grace, and the completion of nature."[12] Each of the three reasons demands the resurrection of the body. The body must rise, first because it – as much as the soul – merits punishment or reward ("rectitude of justice") and is likened to Christ –

---

[11] Ménard, "The Spirituality of *Transitus* ...," 50.
[12] St. Bonaventure, *Breviloquium* Part 7, Ch. 5, par 2, ed. and trans. Dominic Monti, Works of St. Bonaventure IX (St. Bonaventure, NY: Franciscan Institute Publications, 2005), 283.

as much as the soul ("restoration of grace"). Bonaventure's discussion
of the last element of this triad, however, is most evocative for our investigation. The saint explains that "the completion of nature demands
that human beings be constituted of both body and soul, *as matter and
form mutually need and seek each other.*"[13]

This understanding of soul and body mutually seeking each other
is an important aspect of Bonaventure's theology of death. Caroline
Walker Bynum, in her classic study on the resurrection of the body,
maintains that the foundation for Bonaventure's understanding of
bodily resurrection is his understanding of desire.[14] She explains that
for Bonaventure the analogy "is not biological but psychological: the
love of a man for a woman."[15] Bonaventure's argument should be understood as follows: "A complete substance composed of its own form
and matter, soul nonetheless needs body for completion; longing for
body (*appetites, desiderium, inclinatio ad corpus*) is thus lodged in its very
being."[16] Citing his First Sermon on the Feast of the Assumption, she
clarifies that for Bonaventure, "the person is not [only] the soul; it is
a composite." The entrance of Mary into heaven, therefore, must be
"as a composite, that is, of soul and body; otherwise she would not be
in perfect joy."[17] The sermon continues: "body must return to soul in
order for soul to be perfectly blessed."[18] Thus for Bonaventure, after
death – even in heaven – the person will not be completely happy until
the resurrection of the body. The *Breviloquium* explains this point further: "Hence, the soul cannot be fully happy unless a body is restored
to it, because it has an inclination built into it by nature to be reunited
with the body."[19]

One may then extrapolate from this understanding of the soul's
desire to be reunited with the body, as with one who is loved, and ask

---

[13] *Breviloquium*, Part 7, Ch. 5, par 2, 283; emphasis added.

[14] Caroline Walker Bynum, *The Resurrection of the Body in Western Christianity,
1200-1336* (New York: Columbia University, 1995), 248.

[15] Bynum, *The Resurrection of the Body in Western Christianity*, 237.

[16] Bynum, *The Resurrection of the Body in Western Christianity*, 248. Bynum bases
her understanding on Michael Schmaus's "*Die Unsterblichkeit der Seele und die Auferste-
hung des Leibes nach Bonaventure,*" L'Homme et son destin d'après les penseurs du moyen âge,
Actes du premier Congrès International de Philosophie Médiévale, 1958 (Louvain: Nauwe-
laerts, 1960), 505-19.

[17] Bynum, *The Resurrection of the Body in Western Christianity*, 249, n. 77.

[18] Bynum, *The Resurrection of the Body in Western Christianity*, 250.

[19] *Breviloquium*, Part 7, Ch. 7, par 4, 294.

what death as separation of soul and body must mean for Bonaventure. John Saward describes how the decomposition that followed death functioned as a powerful symbol for the saint:

> Bodily death in all its hideousness is not only punishment for sin, it is also, in a certain sense, the terrible symbol of the deformity that is sin. Death is the final ugliness. The body's beauty is destroyed. It decomposes, rots, falls apart. In fact, when no longer informed by the spiritual soul, it is not really a body at all, but a loose amalgam of dissipating elements.... But it is not only the repulsiveness of decomposing flesh that makes death ugly. The separation of immortal soul from mortal body is a marring of the beauty of the whole human nature, which God made to be a unity of matter and spirit. It is a cruel and crude severance. Like St. Thomas, Bonaventure held that the soul separated from the body is not a complete human being.[20]

For Bonaventure death, therefore, is ambiguous. It is the entrance into glory, but it is also an evil in which the soul is most cruelly separated from the body, its lover.[21] Bynum refers to "an astonishing passage of the *Breviloquium* devoted to the crucifixion" in which Bonaventure states that the more perfect a body is, the more fully it experiences.[22] In Christ's passion, therefore, "because his body possessed perfect physical balance and his senses were in their full vigor, and as his soul possessed perfect love for God and supreme concern for neighbor, his anguish in both body and soul was immeasurable."[23] Christ's death itself became the locus of this anguish. Bonaventure maintains:

> [S]ince it is precisely the union of body and soul that makes a living human being, it follows that, during those three days [after his death], Christ was not a man, although both his soul and body were united to the Word. But because death in Christ's

---

[20] John Saward, "The Flesh Flowers Again: St. Bonaventure and the Aesthetics of the Resurrection," *Downside Review* 110 (January 1992): 4-5.

[21] See Bonaventure's sermon on the 15th Sunday after Pentecost. *Opera omnia*, Vol. IX, 411b. For an English translation see *The Sunday Sermons of St. Bonaventure*, introduction, translation and notes by Timothy J. Johnson, WSB XII (St. Bonaventure, NY: Franciscan Institute Publications, 2008), 450.

[22] See Bynum, *The Resurrection of the Body in Western Christianity*, 251.

[23] *Breviloquium*, Part 4, Ch. 9, par 6 (Monti, 163).

human nature could not bring death to the person who never ceases to live, death itself perished in life.[24]

When this second element of Bonaventure's theology of death is added to the first, one sees that dying for a Franciscan is an ambiguous experience: it is the entrance into glory, but at the same time it is being ripped and separated from one's most dear friend. The soul will never be fully happy until it is reunited to the body.

THE FRANCISCAN SPIRITUAL TRADITION: ST. BERNARDINE OF SIENA

If death is an ambiguous concept for the Franciscan theological tradition, how does the Franciscan spiritual look at the same phenomenon? One can find at least part of the answer by investigating the writings of St. Bernardine of Siena (1380-1444). One of the most famous preachers of his day, he devoted at least thirty of his sermons and treatises to the subject of the "Last Things."[25] In these sermons he would remind his congregation that "constant meditation upon death and its aftermath is a necessary and salutary exercise to Christians who want to save their souls."[26]

Living during the historical period that was ravaged by the Black Death, he was preaching to people who saw themselves as living in the shadow of death. He described death to his congregations as "inevitably bitter for all of human kind 'due to our natural condition.'" Yet for the righteous it was also a "release from prison, the end of exile, the termination of life's hard labor, the departure from a ruined house, an escape from all the perils of life, a return to the homeland, the beginning of life, and the entry to eternal glory."[27] An ambivalence

---

[24] *Breviloquium*, Part 4, Ch. 9, par 8 (Monti, 164).

[25] Franco Mormando, "What Happens to Us When We Die? Bernardino of Siena on 'The Four Last Things,'" in DuBruck and Gusick, eds., *Death and Dying in the Middle Ages* (Bern/New York: Peter Lang Publishing Group, 1999), 110. Writings on the "Last Things" dealt with death, judgment, heaven and hell.

[26] Mormando, "What Happens," 110.

[27] Mormando, "What Happens," 111. Mormando is quoting from the sermon of the Friday after the First Sunday of Lent, "*De duodecim doloribus quos patitur peccator in hora mortis.*"

concerning death remains in the Franciscan spiritual tradition, but it is a different sort of ambivalence from that of the theological tradition.

For sinners, however, there is no ambivalence at all concerning death and dying. Preaching in order to change the way people lived their lives, Bernardine described the death of the sinner as "irremediably horrible,"[28] filled with both bodily pain and mental anguish. In his sermon on "The Twelve Afflictions That the Sinner Experiences at the Hour of Death," he is quite graphic in his description. There is no escape from the physical, emotional, and spiritual suffering. Soon the devil will come to lead the person to judgment. Bernardine mimics the devil:

> 'Come, O wretched one, to appear before God.' Oh what terror, what horror, what astonishment when the wretched soul sees these demons prepared to pounce on their prey! O foolish soul, who will protect you in the hour of such great need? Who will console you? Who will stand by you?[29]

It was Bernardine who described the desire to prolong life as stemming from "the foolish belief that one can evade death" and demonstrating an attachment to life that is still "sinfully loved."[30]

Comparing the theological tradition as articulated by Bonaventure and the spiritual tradition as seen in Bernardine, one sees both important similarities and interesting contrasts. For example, when Bernardine speaks of the death of the righteous person, his language is similar to that used by Bonaventure in his description of *transitus*. Likewise, when Bernardine speaks of death as the separation of the soul and body, like Bonaventure, he sees this as part of the anguish and suffering of the dying. But while for Bonaventure this speaks of an appropriate desire that soul and body have for the other that will not be satisfied until the resurrection of the body, this separation is understood very differently by Bernardine. Because the sinner clings to things of this world, it is for this reason that the separation of the

---

[28] Mormando, "What Happens," 112.

[29] *De duodecim doloribus* 1, in *S. Bernardini Senensis Opera Omnia Tomus I, Quadragesimale de Christiana Religione*, ed. Pacifico Perantoni, Works of St. Bernardino of Siena (Florence: Ad Claras Aquas, 1950), 162.

[30] Mormando, "What Happens," 112.

soul from the body is especially painful for the sinner.[31] The impression given by Bernardine is that this would not be the case for the righteous person. Furthermore, given this suffering and pain, the one who is attached to this life may be unable even to make a final proper act of contrition. Bernardine concludes that "it is difficult and almost impossible for the soul to escape and be saved."[32]

CONCLUSION: WHAT CAN THE TRADITION TEACH US ABOUT DYING AS A FRANCISCAN?

What does the tradition say to the followers of Francis and Clare today regarding how one can die as a Franciscan? It would seem that at the very least the tradition calls contemporary Franciscans (1) to retrieve a theological understanding of the afterlife and understand how this theology affects our understanding of end of life care itself and (2) return to a deeper understanding of what it means to care for our seriously ill and dying sisters and brothers.

A Theology of Death

For almost fifty years, many Christians have decried the secularization of the field of medical ethics. Allen Verhey, for example, has challenged contemporary Christian bioethicists "to talk candidly about the difference it makes to be a believer, to speak prophetically concerning the culture, and to draw out the implications for bioethics of such faith and criticism."[33]

The Franciscan tradition may have something prophetic to say about returning to specifically Christian end-of-life care and ethical reflection. Medieval theologians like Bonaventure and Medieval preachers like Bernardine necessarily began their reflections with an explicit theology of death. What would end of life care look like today if its practitioners would articulate such a theology of death and then show how that theology related to their concrete ethics?

---

[31] Mormando, "What Happens," 113. See "De duodecim doloribus," 1, 160.

[32] Mormando, "What Happens," 113. Mormando is quoting from "De duodecim doloribus," 1, 141.

[33] Allen Verhey, Reading the Bible in the Strange World of Medicine (Grand Rapids: Eerdmans Publishing Company, 2003), 20.

Bonaventure's understanding of death as both *transitus* and the painful separation of the soul from the body had concrete ramifications for his understanding of care for the dying and for his belief concerning the suffering one faces at death. Seldom are bioethicists challenged today to articulate their own theology of death and to explain how that understanding explicitly enters into their assessment of end of life decisions. Yet a theology of death as a foundation for end-of-life moral decisions may be more critical today than ever before.

Caring for the Dying

The Catholic ethical tradition regarding the end of life prides itself on being an ethic of care. The *Ethical and Religious Directives for Catholic Health Care Services* state that the Catholic health care institution "as a witness to faith ... will be a community of respect, love and support to patients or residents and their families as they face the reality of death."[34] The Directives go on to remind physicians that the "task of medicine is to care even when it cannot cure."[35] A conversation between the Franciscan tradition and Catholic medical ethics can, however, clarify the true meaning of end-of-life care.

Rooted in the Middle Ages, the Franciscan tradition has not been inclined to equate care simply with the prolongation of life. The tradition arose at a time when many attempts to prolong life were actually seen as immoral and evidence of an attachment to a life that was still "sinfully loved."[36] The Franciscan tradition thus raises larger questions regarding the nature of care for the dying. It asks whether the "medical good" is truly good for a given patient.[37] As end of life decisions become more technological and more complicated, perhaps the Franciscan tradition and the questions it raises can offer clarity amidst the confusion.

---

[34] United States Conference of Catholic Bishops, *Ethical and Religious Directives for Catholic Health Care Services* (Washington, DC: USCCB, 2009), "Introduction to Part Five, Care for the Seriously Ill and Dying."

[35] *Ethical and Religious Directives*, "Introduction to Part Five, Care for the Seriously Ill and Dying."

[36] See Mormando, "What Happens to Us When We Die?" 112.

[37] Richard A. McCormick, *Health and Medicine in the Catholic Tradition* (New York: Crossroad Publishing Company, 1984), 115.

PRAISED BE MY LORD THROUGH SISTER DEATH: A FRANCISCAN SPIRITUALITY OF DYING

MARY PETROSKY, F.M.M.

When the topic for this year's Symposium was first announced as "Dying, as a Franciscan," Anthony Carrozzo, with whom I collaborate in The Franciscan Center for Spirituality and Spiritual Direction, commented to me, "I didn't know that Franciscans died any differently than anyone else!" Anthony likes to tease, but I also took this as a challenge in my presentation. Is there a difference for Franciscans? Should there be a difference? And what would that difference be, not just in death, but more importantly in the life which preceded death.

While the process of dying, physically, emotionally, and intellectually is a universal phenomenon, the experience of dying can be and is most individual. I believe that much of the individuality of the experience can be shaped, nurtured and deeply affected by one's spirituality. Do we, or can we as Franciscans find insights into dying from Francis's life and from his death?

Francis called her Sister Death. I haven't come to fully understand why the word death (in Italian) is feminized, but on further reflection, it became clearer to me that Francis, in calling her Sister Death, revealed his sensitivity to insights from a feminine worldview. I believe Francis saw death as giving birth to new life! Death is a passage – a passage through a "birth canal" which is sometimes difficult and painful. And most often the passage is not achieved without a great amount of pain. That birth canal is our life on earth, and especially those last moments of physical life before entering into eternal life. For that "final push" into eternal life, we pray that Jesus, or Mary, or Francis, or Clare, will be there to encourage us to Push! How many "midwives" have aided us along our passage? How much more feminine in thought could that be? You may find some richness in that visualization as you reflect more on death and of those "midwives" in your own life. Picture them and name them for yourselves.

We preach that death is a passing from one form of life into another form – eternal life with God (whatever that means). Nobody has come back to tell us what that is. I'm not privy to what that is either but I want to share what I have come to believe is important. It is what I have discovered in my own journey and reflections on death as I approach that moment of ecstatic encounter, which I believe in by faith alone.

In my experience with our sisters in the retirement community, in casual conversations, I quickly learned that the approach to dying could be placed on a continuum beginning with: "I want everything to be done that can be done" to an accepting "Please don't prevent me from dying." There are endless possible stages between those two pillars.

What are your thoughts on just the physical aspects of dying? Have you thought about your Living Will? Some of our sisters have almost had to be forced to fill in a form and make some decisions about their wishes in readiness for when serious illness is diagnosed. What are we afraid of? The pain, the process, of course, the great unknown of that, can be frightening. But is there something else, something related to our face-to-face encounter with the God who created us, called us to serve him in this life as a Franciscan, but firstly, and always, as a struggling human being? That along with one's spiritual preparations will be the gristle and the grind of today's input.

My personal insight into death has been fed and enriched by a study and reflection on how Francis came to prepare for and to welcome Sister Death. We Franciscans make a big thing of Francis's death, celebrating it yearly with the Transitus ceremony. Maybe it is a salutary thing for us to look at, recalling Paul's words:

Just as it is appointed that human beings die once, and after this the judgment (Heb 9:27).

The date of death itself is rarely, if ever, known much in advance. But often there are warning signs and harbingers of impending (no, not doom) but of a momentous event – one's own death. I guess we may learn later rather than earlier that preparation for death should find an important place in our own spiritual journey. This develops, I believe, as we spiritually mature into accepting what that first face-to-face encounter with God really means, based on our knowledge of the Scriptures and our reflections on those scriptures and their commentaries.

Certainly, we have been surrounded by death these past few months with the earthquakes in Haiti, in Chile, the wars in Iraq, Afghanistan, and the violence in almost every part of our world. We presently observe the vast destruction of sea life, our waters, and our shores caused by the explosion of the deep sea drilling for oil off the coast of our shores in the Gulf of Mexico. Every death is a reminder of our own – coming we know not when, but we know that it is coming. Hearing of events such as these, I find myself thinking in images of Francis's life and his death.

The image which dominated my thoughts was that of a dying Francis stripped naked lying on the ground at the Portiuncula. Nudity, especially nudity before one's Maker, is the state we know we are all approaching. I prefer to think of this, not as nudity, but more as transparency. I would define transparency as "without gloss" – spiritually, psychologically and physically – that is "what you see is what you get" – the "real thing" sort of genuine frankness and total openness – with not an ounce of pretense – cosmetics, make-up of any kind.

Francis began his growth into total transparency before God when he stripped himself before Bishop Guido, his father, and probably, most of the citizens of Assisi (1C VI:15).[1] We can recall when he stripped himself of his princely armor on the way to Perugia – giving it to a real knight – perhaps the beginning of an awareness of the need to be authentic/transparent (2C II:5).[2]

Maybe this awareness began with the stripping of his outer garments at this early stage. The process of being transformed into the Christ of the Gospels who had pursued him was begun. But it was only the beginning. While starting from the outside, Francis gradually

---

[1] Thomas of Celano, *The Life of Saint Francis*, in *Francis of Assisi: Early Documents*, Vol. 1, ed. Regis Armstrong, O.F.M. Cap., J.A. Wayne Hellmann, O.F.M. Conv., William Short, O.F.M. (New York: New City Press, 1999), 193. Additional citations will be made to *FA:ED* followed by volume and page number.

[2] Thomas of Celano, *The Remembrance of the Desire of a Soul*, in *FA:ED* 2, 244.

began to strip his soul and spirit of all that prevented God from permeating his entire being. He wanted Christ to be his all in all. Adam and Eve, when they sinned, recognized their nakedness, and were given clothes to wear to cover their bodies (Gen 4:21). Certainly they carried within them the knowledge and shame of their disobedience. But the original state of being and of innocence was complete nudity. Since then, creation has been longing to return to that original state. When we think of our own death, how do we prepare to meet our Maker? How do we work back to a state of innocence (transparency)? That sounds so esoteric, but in common terms what we want to do is to clear up, erase, or heal, as we can, the broken relationships, the unfinished business of our lives with others, our world, and with ourselves. I have found that many older people as they face death, are seeking to mend whatever has been broken in their lives.

Let's look again at Francis and what transpired in the years and months just preceding his death. It was on Mt. La Verna, during his retreat in mid-September of the year 1224, that many believe Francis was mystically transformed into the dying Christ, who had been stripped and nailed to a cross before his death.

Although we know that death can be physical, we also know that there can also be deaths of other kinds. Each of us can recall an experience when something within us died. Maybe it was pride, or vanity, or trust in ourselves or in another. Whatever it was, positive or negative, we knew that we were different, transformed in some way. Whatever was gone made us better, or worse, but we were changed in some way by that death.

Francis's growth into total transparency before God probably had its most dramatic movement when Francis was at La Verna the year of his death.[3] This experience is popularly believed to have been the imposition of the wounds known as the Stigmata. Francis had prayed throughout his life to know who God was. The answer came in the dream vision: his God was the God of the abandoned, dying Jesus, to whom he had given his life. With St. Paul, he could say of his sufferings, "I have been crucified with Christ" – the faith alone gave meaning to his agony and redeemed him from the crushing burden of absurdity. "It is no longer I who live," Paul continued, "it is Christ who lives in

---

[3] Donald Spoto, *The Reluctant Saint The Life of Francis of Assisi* (New York: Viking Compass, 2003), 190.

me. And the life I now live in the flesh, I live by faith in the Son of God, who loved me and gave himself for me" (Gal 2:19-20).

With this event, Francis knew the meaning of conformity to Christ in absolute poverty – to accept his own limitations, his own complete reliance on God. As he looked back upon his life, Francis recognized that he was not to be a successful cloth merchant as was his father. Now, he could also recognize that there would be no visible signs of spiritual success. He did not convert the Sultan; he did not suffer martyrdom. The fraternity was not developing as he had planned and formed it. He had tried to imitate the life of Jesus; now, in his decline and approaching death, in his frustrations and failures, he would follow that path all the way to the cross.

At Mt. La Verna in 1224, Francis came at last to understand that the martyrdom he had so avidly sought was to come in an unexpected form. It would come in his abandonment of self to God, his acceptance of diminishment and pain and in the dissolution of his dreams for his companions. Francis was stripping himself of his dreams of glory and accepting, as Christ did, the plan/dream that God had for him. This was a dying to self, allowing the transparency to become more and more pervasive in his entire body and especially in his soul.

On the morning of October 3, 1226, Francis told his caregivers,

When you see that I have come to the end, put me out naked on the ground as you saw me naked the day before yesterday, and once I am dead allow me to lie there for as long as it takes to walk a leisurely mile (2C 217).[4]

That afternoon, they heard him whisper the opening verses of Psalm 141:1.

Lord, I call to you, come quickly to help me;
listen to my plea when I call.

His friends followed his instruction, and placed him stripped on the floor of his cell – it was the full realization of the dramatic moment before Bishop Guido so many years earlier. As he lay dying and the afternoon began to fade, Francis's final prayer was a sublime gesture, his

---

[4] *FA:ED 2*, 388.

ultimate action by which he expressed what he was and whose child he
was, about to be born again in eternity.[5] Francis's intuitive insight expressed when he called Death "Sister Death" was realized. Francis was
born again and this time death brought him birth into Eternal Life.

We recall Francis's words, as recorded in Admonition XIX:

> Blessed is the servant who does not consider himself any bet-
> ter when he is praised and exalted by people than when he is
> considered worthless, simple, and looked down upon, for what
> a person is before God, that he is and no more.[6]

The transparency was realized.

Francis was not afraid to die. In reality Francis welcomed Sister
Death. I think that people who are not afraid of living have a better
chance of not being afraid of dying! While I have spoken much about
death, much also has been said about life. Francis lived his life, before
his conversion, to the full – as a rogue, a rake, a man with friends who
enjoyed good fellowship and good fun with all. He also lived fully after
his conversion, on a different plane, daring to be and to do all that he
could be and do to imitate the life of Jesus Christ. His great respect for
every word in the Scriptures is well documented by his biographers.

Recently I have discovered that the story of Nicodemus in John
3:1-15, emphasizing "being born again," gives added insight into Francis's love of Sister Death, seen as rebirth into eternal life.

The best and only preparation for a "good death" is to live a "good
life." The story of Nicodemus, a Pharisee, is an introduction to a good
man who obviously is a seeker and has recognized goodness in this up-
start preacher "rabbi." How does he recognize him? Nicodemus greets
Jesus with

> Rabbi, we know that you are a teacher who has come from
> God for no one can do the signs which you do unless God is
> with him (John 3:2).

And Jesus' response to this is to say:

---

[5] Spoto, *The Reluctant Saint*, 215.
[6] *FA:ED* 1, 135.

Amen, amen, I say to you, no one can see the kingdom of God without being born from above. This is the truth, I tell you unless a man is born from above, he cannot see the kingdom of God (John 3:3).

We recall the rest of the dialogue where Jesus clarifies Nicodemus' concern about reentering his mother's womb as a grown man. (Certainly many early seekers/converts tended to interpret things literally). I wondered, in reading this, if Jesus were teasing Nicodemus, or testing him! As a Pharisee, Nicodemus took on the all consuming task of spending his life observing every detail of the scribal law. To the Jew the Law was the most sacred thing in the world. The Scribes worked out the regulations re: the Law. The Pharisees dedicated their lives to live it with all the regulations which had been proposed.[7]

Nicodemus was a Pharisee, and it is astonishing that a man who believed goodness and perfection were found by scrupulously following the law and its regulations and that that was what pleased God, would wish to talk to Jesus at all. Yet, he realized that Jesus' healing ministry was surely the work of God.

It was at night that Nicodemus came to Jesus. Was he being cautious – not wanting to be seen by others, conversing with this untried rabbi of questionable origins?

When Nicodemus comes to Jesus, he said that no one could help being impressed with the signs and wonders that he did. Jesus' answer was that it was not the signs and the wonders that were really important; the important thing was such a change in a man's inner life that it could only be described as a new birth.

Here we have again the image of new life, with the imagery of birth, of an entrance into a new life. To be born of water and the spirit, is a new birth into a new life.

When Jesus says:

Do not be amazed that I told you, 'You must be born from above.' The wind blows where it wills, and you can hear the sound it makes, but you do not know where it comes from or

---

[7] William Barclay, *Gospel of John,* Vol. 1 Revised Edition (Philadephia: The Westminster Press, 1975), 120-34.

where it goes. So it is with everyone who is born of the Spirit
(John 3:7).

I believe that Jesus is saying that the man/woman born from above is
a free person, just as free as the wind which blows where it wills. Certainly a follower of Jesus' freedom is led or curtailed only by the love
which the person's penetration by the Spirit inspires.

What should we be fearful of? If we are fearful of death, could it be
that we are also fearful of life? ... fearful of the possibility of using the
freedom which the invasion of the Spirit offers?

Nicodemus is a seeker, we can conjecture THAT from his approach to Jesus. He comes in the night, but he is obviously seeking the
light. He comes to be instructed although his life has been dedicated
to living out every dot and title of the Law. Obviously something is
urging him on to a bigger world, a larger horizon, having heard and
possibly witnessed the freedom of Jesus to perform works of God and
yet to be a person of the Law.

Nicodemus has the courage to come to Jesus and the humility to
ask Jesus for enlightenment. He recognizes the freedom with which
Jesus is following the Law and his freedom in interpreting that law
when people approach him with a need for healing even on the Sab-
bath! He sees that Jesus responds always to the need of the other –
whether a physical or a moral need for healing.

How many births take place in a person's life? There can be countless ones for each of us depending upon our courage, our daring and
our faith in Jesus who came to free us.

Nicodemus is an excellent example of a man struggling to experience the fullness of life. Our talk today was also of our struggle to
experience life in it fullness. We are speaking of all of life, physical life,
emotional life, intellectual life, in our youth, life in middle age, and life
in our later years, but especially eternal life, the life we were born to
experience. And we reach it through many births.

G.K. Chesterton has a wonderful description of Francis of Assisi
which gives insight into how Francis lived. It reminds me so much of
what Jesus was trying to teach Nicodemus.

Chesterton says of Francis:

St. Francis was a lean and lively little man, thin as a thread and vibrant as a bowstring. In appearance he must have been like a thin brown skeleton autumn leaf dancing eternally before the wind: *but in truth it was he that was the wind.*

Francis teaches us much about Death, but also much about Life. Francis knew the freedom of the wind in both life and death. Francis knew how to die because Francis knew how to live.

"I Beg All My Brothers and Sisters Not to be Disturbed or angry in their infirmities": Transition and Loss at the End of Life

Mary Petrosky, F.M.M.

I've learned many things throughout my life especially from living in and with other cultures. During my years in Papua New Guinea, I came to appreciate the New Guineans' use of inductive reasoning. We westerners go from the general to the particular (deductive), while most often the New Guineans move from the particular to the general. Our brothers and sisters in transition are very much in the inductive mode! Transition is very particular to each one.

In presenting this session there is great value in using these two approaches to transition. I will present a particular experience of transition at our retirement center in Providence, Rhode Island which took place in the mid-90s. Kate will focus on three important aspects/ingredients of a healthy transition: 1. Mindfulness, 2. Wisdom, 3. Transparency – in all of life, which certainly prepare one for the particular transitions of life. How do we help our brothers and sisters to accept the new ministry of aging, not ministry to the aging?

What are some of the practical aspects of bringing others, and ourselves, to the point of accepting that the diminishment which is happening in our bodies, our minds, and our spirits, calls us to enter into a new phase of our lives? This transition most often means less physical activity with the gradual (if not sudden) withdrawal from the ministries which gave us life.

Transition probably begins with part-time, or limited involvement in ministry and eventually to total withdrawal (retirement). Then comes the move to a retirement community, or an Assisted Living community and then to a Nursing Home, if needed. The person who chooses or accepts such a transfer will adjust more easily than the one who has been obliged to make the transfer (due to physical or mental condition) and may be in denial of the need.

Staffing of our facilities to which the person is transferred is extremely important. Our administrators spend much time, effort and finances to hire competent staff who are imbued with a Franciscan joy and compassion.

Sometimes our cleaning staff are the people who best exhibit this quality to our residents. Many of our staff members are new immigrants to this country and know what it means to come into a new environment, even world, so different from what they had previously known. Our residents are now in a "new world" from the one in which they had previously served.

One of the greatest challenges for a newly arrived brother or sister, and for the staff, is to provide, not only loving and competent care, but to encourage and support the resident in as much productive activity as is possible. I have witnessed that the most difficult adjustment for the newly arrived brother or sister, is to have nothing to "get out of bed for." The sister or brother, if still able to contribute something from the wisdom and riches of his or her life or experiences, should be encouraged and enabled to do so. Assisted Living facilities differ greatly from that of nursing home settings. Each situation brings a unique and difficult challenge to the staff. The physical and emotional health of each resident is the basic consideration for the possibility of some limited involvement in ministry.

One very important ministry for the residents is the ministry of prayer. At our assisted living facility in Providence, RI, the telephone receptionist and many of the sisters in residence remark how frequently requests are received from neighbors, families, friends.

The community at large views the monastery/convent as a "powerhouse of prayer." And the sisters and brothers diligently and seriously respond to these requests.

In the mid-nineties, we F.M.M. had the experience of transferring twenty of our sisters from our "Infirmary" (as it was first called in the

30s) to a Nursing home, operated by the diocese of Providence. We were unable to be licensed as a nursing home facility for many reasons, mainly due to stringent restrictions for nursing home facilities re: fire codes, sprinkler systems, etc.

There was much preparation of/and/with the twenty sisters who were to be transferred. For three months, weekly meetings were held to prepare the sisters for this move. During these sessions, the sisters were invited to voice their concerns, questions, express their anger, some feeling that they were being "put out" at this stage of their lives. At the same time, staff worked with them to sort out and prepare what clothing or items they would be taking with them.

As a missionary Institute, we have placed a great emphasis on "Sending and Receiving" as two of the most important aspects of our missionary lives. This was another sending for the sisters and in a simple but deeply moving ceremony in our chapel, the sisters were missioned by the Provincial to St. Antoine Nursing Center in No. Smithfield, RI. As the Province plans Mission-sending ceremonies when sisters are missioned to other countries, this was presented as a sending to ministry to others in a new situation, and a new culture. Each sister was given a candle and an icon of Mary, which had been painted by one of our artists. Representatives of the Nursing Home staff were present for the ceremony. It was a deeply moving occasion for all and never forgotten by those of us who attended.

A small community of F.M.M.s was established in a private home across the road from St. Antoine's. These three sisters were missioned also to minister to the sisters in residence, not to do nursing care, but to assure the sisters that they were not sent away and forgotten. Each week sisters from the Providence address visit the sisters at St. Antoine's.

Kate will now share with you from her experience and her insights into the stages of transition which she has found to be useful in working with the retired members of her community. You may want to be thinking about these stages of transition in light of the example you have just heard.

I BEG ALL MY BROTHERS AND SISTERS, ETC. ...

KATHLEEN McCARRON, O.S.F.

I thought I would begin this talk with a poem by David Whyte entitled "The Journey."[1] So, take a deep breath and think about the journey.

> Above the mountain,
> the geese turn into the light again
> Painting their black silhouettes on an open sky
> Sometimes everything has to be inscribed above the heavens
> So that you can find the one line already written inside you.
> Sometimes it takes a great sky
> to find that freedom
> to find that first bright and indescribable wedge of freedom in your
>   own heart.
> Sometimes with the bones of the black stick left when the fire has
>   gone out
> Someone has written something new
> in the ashes of your life.
> You are not leaving even as the lights fade quickly; you are arriv-
>   ing.

So how do I prepare for this holy arriving? It is both an active and a passive preparation. The active art of arriving might best be considered in light of our life's transitions. It seems to me that it would be very helpful to reflect on one's life's transitions and to glean information about oneself during these periods. Was I the catalyst of the tran-

---

[1] David Whyte, "The Journey," in *House of Belonging* (Langley, WA: Many Rivers Press, 1997).

sition? Was I the conduit through which the transition occurred? Or was I merely affected by the transition? As Franciscans when we pause to examine these periods, we view them in the context of the deep relationship which God maintains with each of us. Thus, we will discover that in our transitions we are not alone. God is with us continually teaching us about ourselves. As we move closer to our own homecoming, what are the signs that we have made successful life transitions?

Three words came to my heart when I was thinking about this for our consideration—mindfulness, wisdom and transparency. Mindfulness leads to integrity and authenticity. It is not just looking inward. It is a matter of being fully present to each step in life. To let what comes, come, to pause and be with the events of my life; to sit with my personal story, to experience integration of these events and to be authentically who God is calling me to be. And I thought of Francis withdrawing in prayer frequently to sit and experience how the hand of God was working in his life. Thus, as we approach death mindfully we are able to embrace the limitations of our life as well as our strengths. It is not a matter of making sense out of it all. It is a matter of seeing and experiencing how the hand of God is at work within me just as Francis did. If I approach my life transitions in a mindful stance then when I stand in the truth of my own mortality I live in such a way that I have a clear understanding of where my life is going.

Wisdom is the second characteristic achieved through successful transitioning. A person gains wisdom through experience over time. The wise person possesses the perspective from which the unintegrated units of life can be linked, understood and accepted at their deepest levels. Wisdom leads to self-awareness. In the words of the poet, Henry David Thoreau I quote, "It is as hard to see oneself as to look backwards without turning around." Thus, if we give wisdom a chance so to speak; if we let go of our judgmental ways, our preconceived notions of this is how things are to be done, if we approach life with a Franciscan stance of outstretched arms, palms upturned and pause and reflect on the sum total of our experiences, we move forward in wisdom with a clarity about our feelings, our beliefs and our actions, and God is present in each of these.

The third aspect obtained by successful transitioning is that of transparency. As I move towards my final transitus or transition, I realize that my story is nestled in the story of the universe. I am part of something much bigger than myself. I bring my true self to the moment—my brokenness, my limitations, my inability to reach beyond myself. In humility, I also bring my talents, my life successes, and my yearning heart. I have the sense of where I've been and where I'm going. In transparency, I realize that God continues to call me to life until my last breath. So I thought we could just take a minute here to pause and reflect on our own personal life transition. Just close your eyes and be reflective on this. I am going to ask you not to judge yourselves. Simply see if there are any patterns. Notice how you handle them. Maybe just take a stand as, "Isn't that curious?" See if you were the catalyst, if you were the conduit, or simply affected by transition. So just take a minute.

So, as we examine our life transitions, we see them in the context of the many conversions that God has called us to along the way. Each time we have experienced loss and we grieve that loss and face our feelings and honor them, each time we allow God to grace us with new life and new relationships, we experience conversion and it happens over and over and over again in the course of our lives. And so it is with our final conversion, our dying and our death. The center of our Franciscan call is a life of conversion of heart, and the real heart of the matter is our final conversion, our final turn from life as we know it to the fullness of life, eternal life. We have all walked through a number of conversions which have opened us up to new graces throughout our lives, much like labor pains. All of us have learned from childhood that from the minute we are born, we begin to die. And we accept that fact as true and it is certainly true that who we are and what we are still becoming helps change our attitude towards dying. In many ways, it is a consoling fact that we are still in the process of conversion and we can still learn and shape and prepare even when we are entering fully at this time of life into our preparation for eternal life.

Let us look at some of the ways that we can prepare ourselves to meet this God of love. Let me just name a few stages that we might go through in our life. The first is "remote preparation." This is followed by the "retirement phase." The next phase I call "soul time," then the actual "dying" process, and "death" itself. Throughout these phases, the underpinning is conversion, ever turning towards God which is our ongoing life process.

In the remote preparation stage we might give death some thought or we might not; but it seems far off. We are usually engaged in active ministry. Our health is good or at least fair. After all, death happens to others, those who are older or aged. So our preparation may take the form of losing someone we love and thus we begin to think about death.

As we move into the retirement phase, we begin to settle into a different rhythm and at this reflective stance in life we may experience some fear. There is a distinct possibility that fear becomes more vivid in this phase. Why? Because some of our siblings or close friends may be dying. It is no longer our parents, our grandparents, our great aunts and uncles who are dying or those older or frailer than us. So what feelings emerge within us? What emotions do you believe most people carry with them towards their own death and dying? Just think about that for a second. What emotions do you believe most people carry with them towards their own death and dying? Perhaps fear, perhaps separation, perhaps anxiety, perhaps loss of control, perhaps aloneness. The list can go on and on and be as different as each person in this room. It might be helpful at this stage when we are with others and looking at ourselves to make a list of our own fears. Allow it to be a source of revelation to yourself. It may suggest that you need to deal with these fears now. It may suggest that you talk with a friend or a companion on the journey to help you begin dealing with these feelings and these emotions. The purpose of helping others and of dealing with our emotions and feelings now is so that they do not block other supportive emotions that are needed on the journey. An example of this would be people who are struggling when they are dying. They have excessive fear, or they have excessive anxiety and this becomes so pervasive that it blocks out the supportive emotions of joy, of peace, of tranquility.

Retirement is a special time; we move from active ministry to a ministry of presence, a ministry of prayer and a ministry of witness in a new way. We slowly move into the phase where sometimes the lines are blurred as we experience more physical, emotional or psychological diminishment. This catapults us into a more immediate preparation and phase that I call soul time. God uses the normal losses of our later years to help us disengage from the total involvement in the world. At this time of life, we are gifted with time, the precious gift of time which we did not have when we were younger and in a more active ministry. It becomes more natural to be removed from the center of activity especially if we are listening to our bodies, which is another of God's voices. The soul time is a real time for deepening our relationship with God. To be Franciscan is to be in relationship, first with God and then with others and all of creation. So it is a time to be our best selves and it is time to be our truest selves. It is a time to reflect on your life. It is a time to rejoice in the beauty of your soul and your life. It is a time to remember the times you have touched other people's lives and the times they have added joy to yours. It is a time to recall the people who you love and who have loved you. It is a time to thank God for the beauty of the Earth that has enriched your soul and your understanding of God, and it is a time for healing and forgiveness.

As we move through the final phase of skilled care, medical assistance and/or hospice, and move toward our actual dying, it is a time to learn how to be in quiet listening with God. Thus, we are preparing to move from this love relationship with him to the fullness of love and eternal life. This is our final conversion, the heart of the matter, to be in the embrace of the beloved.

SHE CARED FOR HER SICK SISTERS ...

KATHLEEN McCARRON, O.S.F.

I thought I'd begin this talk with another poem by David Whyte. The poem is entitled *The Faces at Braga*.

> In monastery darkness by the light of one flashlight the old shrine
> room waits in silence
> While above the door we see the terrible figure, fierce eyes de-
> manding, "Will you step through?"
> And the old monk leads us, bent back nudging blackness prayer
> beads in the hand that beckons.
> We light the butter lamps and bow, eyes blinking in the pungent
> smoke, look up without a word,
> see faces in meditation, a hundred faces carved above, eye lines
> wrinkled in the hand held light.
> Such love in solid wood! Taken from the hillsides and carved in si-
> lence they have the vibrant stillness of those who made them.
> Engulfed by the past they have been neglected, but through smoke
> and darkness they are like the flowers
> we have seen growing through the dust of eroded slopes, their
> slowly opening faces turned toward the mountain.
> Carved in devotion their eyes have softened through age until their
> mouths curve through delight of the carvers hand.
> If only our own faces would allow the invisible carver's hand to
> bring the deep grain of love to the surface.
> If only we knew as the carver knew, how the flaws in the wood led
> his searching chisel to the very core,

we would smile, too and not need faces immobilized by fear and
the weight of things undone.
When we fight with our failing we ignore the entrance to the
shrine itself and wrestle with the guardian, fierce figure on the
side of good.
And as we fight our eyes are hooded with grief and our mouths are
dry with pain.
If only we could give ourselves to the blows of the carver's hands,
the lines in our faces would be the trace lines of rivers
feeding the sea where voices meet, praising the features of the
mountain and the cloud and the sky.
Our faces would fall away until we, growing younger toward death
every day, would gather all our flaws in celebration
to merge with them perfectly, impossibly, wedded to our essence,
full of silence from the carver's hands.[1]

I chose this poem by David Whyte because I believe that it invites
us into a space which is very Franciscan as we consider caring for our
own. It invites us to allow the hand of the invisible carver to bring the
deep grains of love to the surface; thus, it implies, there is a deep love
within each of us waiting to be unleashed. Even in those among us who
are a little more difficult to love. We are also invited to consider how
the flaws in the wood led the carver's searching chisel to the very core.
Thus, we are called to acknowledge our own flaws and place them in
the hands of the carver.

I would like to suggest that in order to be with those of our own
who are suffering and/or dying, we need to consider our own dying
and rising that occurs in our lives each day. I can't be with anyone until
I have taken stock of myself. Each of us has had multiple experiences
of dying and rising throughout our lives. These experiences may have
been in relationships, in our community living, with authority figures,
with the church, within our families. Perhaps it was a difficult diagno-
sis. Perhaps it was even looking for a ministry and not being able to
find one. Perhaps it was being terminated from a position. Whatever
the experience it transforms us, and we emerge as it were just a little
different from when we entered the process. It is a letting go; it is ac-

---

[1] David Whyte, *The Faces at Braga* (Langley, WA: Many Rivers Press, 1990), 25-27.

knowledging our powerlessness and a willingness to be transformed, trusting the spirit within you and growing in an awareness of where God is leading. Thus, our own experience of dying and rising makes us more compassionate towards our own.

I'd like to quote Ilia Delio here to fully illustrate this point from her book, *Clare of Assisi, A Heart Full of Love*, and I quote,

> Clare had a real sense that death is the path of life. We might say the coming to our real identity means undergoing little deaths that peel away the wires of false self that hide the true self within. To become who we are truly in God, we must die along the way—not once, but many times—a lifetime of little deaths.[2]

We have all had a lifetime of little deaths. So I just want to take a minute here to reflect on that. Simply choose one experience. Think of how you chose to acknowledge it at the time. Remember how you sat with the experiential reality of the concern. Remember what brought you inner peace. Remember what sustained you in your rising. By that, I mean, what moved you from a place of concern, or darkness or anxiety to a place of trust in God. That is your rising. I would like you to take a minute to think of that and then I'm going to ask you to lean into one other person and share what sustained you in your rising. What moved you from a place of darkness to a place of trust in God?

I would suggest that what you shared about what sustained you will be most helpful to you in caring for your own because unless we get in touch with our own feelings, we can't help our companions or anyone on the journey in the art of letting go.

There is a Hindu story that illustrates this point of letting go and transformation that I would like to share. It is the story of a wave. Now the wave is out in the ocean doing exactly what waves do—crashing into boats, swelling, reflecting sunlight and simply sailing along towards the shoreline. As a little wave approaches the beach, she notices that the ones before her seem to crash into the shoreline and then mysteriously disappear. The little wave becomes very frightened. As her turn comes toward the shore she braces herself and crashes into

[2] Ilia Delio, *Clare of Assisi, A Heart Full of Love* (Cincinnati, OH: Saint Anthony Messenger Press, 2007).

the shoreline. Only then does she discover that she's being pulled out, transformed, as it were, and she now recognizes that she is part of the vast ocean. We are very much like that little wave. We are called to let go and enter into the reality of the present, the reality of now. That is how we experience transformation and trust in God. And that is how we allow ourselves to see the infinite possibility even in our dying.

I would like to talk a little bit about the respect and the dignity of the individual, and I've used the book of David Kessler, and his book is entitled, *The Needs of the Dying*. In this book, he lists the needs of the dying. And I'd like to share those with you. The needs of the dying[3] by David Kessler are as follows:

- The need to be treated as a living human being.
- The need to maintain a sense of hopefulness, however changing its focus may be.
- The need to be cared for by those who can maintain a sense of hopefulness, however changing this may be.
- The need to express feelings and emotions about death in one's own way.
- The need to participate in all decisions concerning one's care.
- The need to be cared for by compassionate, sensitive, knowledgeable people who will attempt to understand one's needs.
- The need to expect continuing medical care, even though the goal may change from "cure" to "comfort."
- The need to have all questions answered honestly and fully.
- The need to seek spirituality.
- The need to be free of physical pain.
- The need to express feelings and emotions about pain in one's own way.
- The need of children to participate in death.
- The need to understand the process of death.
- The need to die.
- The need to die in peace and dignity.
- The need not to die alone, and finally,

---

[3] David Kessler, *The Needs of the Dying: A Guide for Bringing Hope, Comfort, and Love to Life's Final Chapter* (New York: Harper Collins, 2000), ix. The original hardcover printing of this text by David Kessler was titled "The Rights of the Dying."

- The need to expect that the sanctity of the body will be respected after death.

If we honor these rights to the best of our ability and in our own way, then I believe that our loved ones will have fully lived until their last breath. One of our sisters said to me when asked "what was the hardest part of this for you?" in the dying process. And she replied, "They look at me in the past tense." First right of the dying, the right to be treated as a living human being, and she said, "They look at me in the past tense." I think there's a really important lesson for each one of us here. We are called to see them as they are. It may not be pretty but to see them as they are. Ask questions; engage them, "what is going on in your life? What are you feeling? What is it like now?" Keep it in the "now" if you can because the "what ifs" create so much anxiety and sometimes just unnecessary anxiety. So try to keep it in the present.

As we care for our own, I encourage each of us to have initial and ongoing conversations about death. Do this formally and do this informally. Many times formal input, such as a talk, a homily, a tape, an article, a piece of music or a piece of art, can be a springboard for a deeper and more intimate conversation with the one for whom we are caring. One example of this not happening occurred when a sister said to me, "No one talks to me about death and what comes next. It's as if they think I really don't know what's going on." So, again the conversation needs to be started and it needs to be ongoing. So say to this person, "Do you experience God with you now? What is your experience of God? How does that relate to how you are feeling today? What is important to you at this phase of life?" The important goal is to evoke a response and more importantly to listen to what is being said or not said. To listen, to listen with our hearts to those for whom we are caring.

There's a story that I think illustrates this very well. I believe the setting is in the late 50s or early 60s when Elisabeth Kübler-Ross was a new physician. The floors of the hospital at that time were set up in such a way that most of the patients filled the rooms near the nurses' station and as a new patient came in, they assigned them rooms going down the hall. However, those patients who were terminal were often placed at the end of the hall, the last rooms at the end of the hall, keeping them from patients who had some hope. Elisabeth would begin her rounds early in the day and many times she would begin with the terminal patients and work her way down the hall. When she went to see these patients, she often noticed that they did not have a spark in their eyes. They exhibited flat affect and were not engaging. One day she was delayed in making her round and as she approached the patients at the end of the hall, she noticed that they had a glimmer in their eyes and they were engaging her. She reflected back to the patients that they seemed to be having a better day and then she began to make observations regarding who came and went in the patients' rooms. It soon became evident that the housekeepers were the consistent people who visited daily to clean the patients' rooms. They often inquired of the patient, "how are you feeling today?" as they were mopping the floor. "Did you have a good night sleep? Did anybody come to visit you? How are you doing with this food?" Having no formal agenda, the housekeepers simply listened to the patients. This was the key for Kübler-Ross. The patients were in a better space personally because someone, in this case, the housekeepers took the time to listen. Thus, it is really vital that we listen to our brothers and our sisters to what they are saying and also what they are not saying. Involve the person as much as possible in all phases of decision-making. Clearly ask and record what the brother or the sister wants or doesn't want as he or she moves towards death. Find out what's important to the individual. Honor the fact that each person has a unique way of dying. There's no uniform way to die. So we need to follow the patient's lead.

There's a delicate balance here that we must maintain when caring for our own. It is a stepping back and allowing the other to be transformed; allowing them to be as involved as they want to be. It might be a help here to listen to the words of Lao Tsu in his book. It's about balance.

> If you want to become whole, let yourself be partial; if you want to become straight, let yourself become crooked; if you want to become full, let yourself be empty; if you want to be reborn, let yourself die; if you want to be given everything, give everything up.[4]

---

[4] Lao-tzu, *Tao Te Ching*, Verse 22, translated by S. Mitchell, (1995).

It is our responsibility caring for our own, to help them identify what is needed now, to help the ongoing transformative conversions that are taking place in their lives until they take their last breath. Again, engage them; ask questions, during this time in your life, "What do you need from others, from us that are caring for you so that you can feel strong emotionally, psychologically, spiritually? How can others, how can we who are caring for you help you find more peace? It might also be a time to work on forgiveness and healing. Are there any past regrets that you could put to rest at this time?" It also might be a time to consider how people want their days defined. Some like to be surrounded by others. Some want no visitors or undesignated visitors. And it is finding the balance of how to enter in, touch them so to speak and lose sight and let them have their space. So it's a very delicate balance for caregivers. Some may want soft music in their room. Some have already asked for that; some may want family pictures, something that is a memory, a community or a constitution; they want to be surrounded by things that are dear to them. That's okay; The rooms where people die do not have to be sterile rooms. It can really be about them. Some of them request that those standing watch pray aloud a rosary or some other favorite prayer. Others may say, "We want to be quiet, stand in quiet prayer with us." Taking care of our own in the spirit of Francis and Clare is to be in touch with our feelings and emotions and then listen with our hearts to the ones who are making their wishes known and then simply step back and follow their lead.

At this point, let's look briefly at working with nursing homes or the staff when we have to place someone at a nursing home or with our families. This could be a community-owned nursing home or an outside facility or a hospice with nurses coming in or those coming to the home to render services. It really is important to communicate with the staff the wishes of the individual. What are the wishes of the individual? It's very important to communicate that. Secondly, especially if it's not our own nursing home, it may be necessary to explain our philosophy of dying. And sometimes even in our own nursing home, it is necessary to explain our philosophy of dying to avoid its becoming "business as usual." So we need to keep refreshing that. Sometimes staff has worked with individuals for a long time. They become like family, they see themselves as family, although we may not see them like that. So being sensitive to their needs and checking on how they are, how they are doing is also important. What you are doing makes a difference; it does. And that kind of engaging can only support them and help them provide better care for the people that we love.

In this sense, after a death, it can be important to provide an outlet for staff and opportunities for them to share their feelings in informal ways so that they can really talk about the person for whom they have cared. Providing formal opportunities, specifically for staff, to remember and ritualize, separate from the funeral, is also important. Continue to check in with them. It's an ongoing process of tapping into people's feelings to see how they are coping. As we grieve, remember that everyone grieves differently. At the wake services, provide time for people to share.

Funeral liturgies should be as personal as possible. Use storyboards to make it personal for the community and family of the deceased. One of our sisters (from Philadelphia and with ties to the Mummer's string bands) wanted her casket led into the chapel with the Mummer's string band leading the way. So, in fact, that happened. And it was very interesting. It was the first and only time that it happened, but it was a request and it was honored. In all their regalia complete with feathers the Mummers played "When the Saints Come Marching In," and led the casket in and out of the Chapel. But her wishes were honored and it was great.

After the funeral ritual it's important to continue to provide opportunities for those who live in the residence to have focused conversations. It's really hard for them. Those of us who minister with them get to go home at the end of the day. They, however, are still in the same environment. It can be very hard for people. So it's important to communicate with them about their grieving.

Another way to have people remember is a necrology. Using a formal necrology for liturgy, or the office, recalling the names of the sisters and the priests or the brothers who have died that day is a significant way to keep their memories alive. For the living, it's a wonderful, wonderful tribute to think about those who have gone before to prepare a place for us.

In closing, one priest that I know has suggested that he would like to be carried out of church with the music from *This Majestic Land*, by Michael Hoppe.[5] It's an instrumental and I am just going to invite you to close your eyes and reflect on being carried out of the church yourself and be peaceful.

---

[5] Michael Hoppé, *This Majestic Land*, released on the Spring Hill Music Label in 2003 and available for listening and viewing on various social networking internet sites.

When the Hour of his Passing was Approaching – Ethical Issues in Care at the End of Life

Daniel Sulmasy, O.F.M., M.D., Ph.D.

We are going to be taking a look at a different technicality. When we talk about death we are going to take a few steps back before death. And I must offer this disclaimer: these are my views and do not represent the opinions of the Presidential Commission for the Study of Bioethical Issues.

I'm going to talk about ethical issues when you're caring for people at the end of life within the Catholic tradition. For many of you this is going to be a review, but I want to make sure everybody's up to speed. We start with some bedrock principles in the sense that everyone is created in the image and the likeness of God and that includes people who are dying. This dignity is an exalted value – a little less than the angels – and is truly inalienable – cannot be taken away by anybody or given away by anyone.

What is most radically equal about us is the fact that we are human and we have a duty to be good stewards of the body. One of the prayers this morning mentioned that no matter how genetic engineering may improve your life, life is always a gift. We cannot choose our own biological parents since it's metaphysically impossible. Life is always given to us and we ought, when our pastors talk to us about stewardship, realize that it's not all about money but also about being good stewards of our bodies. This is the ethical principle behind prevention and doing what our mothers told us – to eat spinach and exercise out of respect for the gift of our bodies – because we have roles to play in the world and duties toward other people and we have obligations that derive from that. But it's a limited duty because while we have this great gift with this wonderful value that we call dignity, we are also finite. We are finite morally, that's the nature of sin; we are finite mentally – we make mistakes and exercise poor judgment; and we are finite physically. And that's who we are as human beings. We have this great exalted value – a little less than the angels – but yet are finite, finite creatures.

Suffering is an experience that makes explicit the inherent tension between this intrinsic dignity and our finitude. Every drop of blood, every wave of nausea, every creek in the bones reminds us of our finitude. Pain and suffering are not the same things. I am the ultimate non-runner but I understand that people like to run marathons. That hurts a lot, but runners seem to enjoy it, so pain is not suffering for them. Yet we also know that there is a lot of suffering that is not physical, such as interpersonal hurt or depression. There is no physical pain there, but still it's deep, deep suffering. Then there's the pain of arthritis. Arthritis in some ways doesn't become suffering until it limits our ability to do what we used to do. It's this tension between being a little less than the angels and yet recognizing that we are finite. It's the tension between those two that's made explicit in an experience that's the occasion of suffering.

Illness is a fact of life but it's also a mystery. People ask the questions all the time, "Why must I suffer, or why must this happen to me or to my child?" It is no accident that many of the great saints have had their experiences of conversion in their own experience of suffering and that of others. Saul of Tarsus was knocked off his horse and blinded yet somehow in this experience hears the voice of God. In our own tradition Francis of Assisi began his conversion experience with his illness as a prisoner of war and extended that experience when he reached out to another who is sick, finally culminating in his embrace of Sister Death.

The goals of medicine really are to minister to this mystery of the human between our dignity and our finitude. That's Right Square where we are. Any of us who are caregivers are putting our hands into the midst of that tension and that mystery. The goals of medicine – stated very well from a medieval perspective – are: to cure sometimes, to relieve often and to comfort always. It's a wonderful phrase that many of us were taught in medical school and promptly forgot because technology makes us physicians feel pretty powerful. We sometimes think we can cure often, and relieve usually. The sad experience of too many patients now is that medicine only comforts when we practitioners get around to it. Technology has relegated comfort to something adjunctive and not central to the goals of medicine as it was in medieval times. And while this technology is wonderful, bypass surgery and CAT scans, and I use them for my own patients, still all that these things seem to bring with them are great burdens.

One of those burdens is iatrogenesic suffering. Iatros is Greek for doctor; so iatrogenic suffering is that caused by doctors. Our medications often have side effects. We see people go through chemotherapy, for instance, or who have had the experience of being on a ventilator. These things can be very difficult for a patient. But this, ironically, highlights another burden that we haven't talked about – the burden of making decisions. If there weren't a ventilator, no one would have to make a decision whether to use it or not. If there weren't dialysis, no one would have to make a decision whether to use it. These decisions put great burdens on patients and also family members.

But don't let anybody ever tell you that Hippocrates is the reason that modern medicine over treats patients. It isn't the Hippocratic Oath that says you have to burden every patient with every available treatment. Neither does it insist "better dead than leukemic!" Hippocrates says nothing of the sort. The oath that I swore says that I will use medical measures to the best of my ability, keeping my patients from harm. That's what it says. And elsewhere in the Hippocratic corpus Hippocrates says this to all physicians, "refuse to treat those who are overmastered by their diseases recognizing that in such cases medicine is powerless."[1] Hippocrates understood what we sometimes have forgotten in the twenty-first century: that medicine is also a finite craft. The function of medicine, as the theologian Paul Ramsey once put it, is not to relieve the human condition of the human condition.[2]

Before that, how many of you have watched Chicago Hope and ER reruns? What do you think that the survival rate is of cardiopulmonary resuscitation on those TV shows? No, it's not 100%; the shows were more realistic. Some colleagues of mine watched a full season of these shows to count up all the resuscitation rates and it was 80%.

---

[1] Hippocrates, *The Art*, iii, 8-10.
[2] Paul Ramsey, as quoted in Courtney S. Campbell, "Religion and The Moral Meaning of Medicine," Hastings Center Report 20, suppl. (July/August, 1990): 4-10..

Here is, in fact, the reality. Out of 100 patients whose heart stopped in the hospital, only 50% of cases will be successfully restarted. Again, starting from that 100, only eighteen are going to make it out of the hospital alive. If you make it out of the hospital alive, at six months only 12% will be alive. So you do pretty well there.

Survival After In-Hospital Arrest

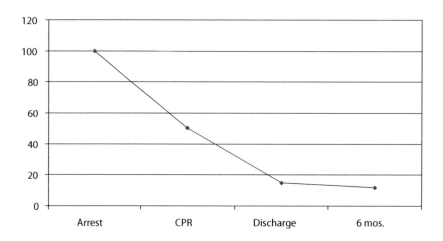

This is a complicated process that is not very effective when people are actually dying of underlying diseases. It was invented for people who are otherwise young and healthy and who get struck by lightning or whose hearts stop suddenly and can be resuscitated. But we seem to apply it reflexively to people who are otherwise dying and it has not gotten any better. This is twelve years of experience of survival. It's flat over the last decade or more. So we are not getting any better at doing that in the hospital.

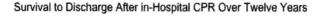

Survival to Discharge After in-Hospital CPR Over Twelve Years

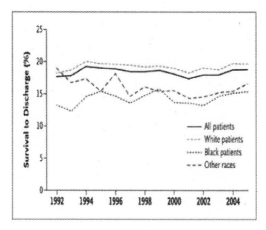

Ehlenbach et al. NEJM 2009;361:22-31

So if we are practicing Hippocratic medicine – Hippocratic healthcare – then an order not to resuscitate, the "DNR" order ought to be regarded as good medicine, not defeat. Our function is not to keep everyone alive for as long as possible. But instead, our function should be a frank recognition that when we come to a patient for whom medicine is powerless then it's time to comfort and to let nature take its course. It's not defeat. Otherwise, we would all be unsuccessful all the time since every patient eventually dies. But, too often, in the hospital it is as if the DNR order becomes the secular last rites. When we finally acknowledge that the patient is dying it is not the end of the conversation but actually the beginning. It's then that we have to talk about proper care for patients and thinking about the proper use of technology at the end of life. We can withhold and withdraw life sustaining treatments other than cardiopulmonary resuscitation.

This is where the Catholic Church has centuries and centuries of wisdom. In fact we invented these words 400 years ago – before there was a word "bioethics" – when people would ask their confessors, "The doctor told me that I'm a poor peasant and they told me that I need to move from Sicily to the Alps for my health." And the wise confessor said, "Well, you don't have to listen to your doctors all the time. You have to be a good steward of your body, but tell me more." And the guy would say, "Well, if I did that I would have to go alone because I couldn't afford to go with my family and then I leave them back here penniless and that seems a lot to keep me alive because the air is better in the Alps. Do I have to do it?" And the wise confessor said, "Well you have an ordinary obligation to use ordinary means to keep yourself alive and be a good steward of your body but there are certain things that you could be asked to do, even by doctors, that are an extraordinary burden, and they are, in fact, optional."

So the first point to make sure that you're clear about is that these words are actually technical, theological terms. They are not words that have their common language meaning of "extraordinary." They do not only mean treatments that have a lot of bells and whistles. Something that is extraordinary means that it is actually optional. It's something that you do not have to do. And any kind of treatment becomes optional either if it's of no benefit or if the burdens are disproportionate to the benefits. And you have to think about this in particular circumstances and not make prior judgments about particular technologies being always ordinary or always extraordinary.

Let's give an example. If any of you were to get a severe attack of appendicitis right now and your appendix were to burst, you'd be taken to the hospital and you would want to have surgery. And when they perform surgery like that, they have to paralyze you. And what happens when you are paralyzed? You stop breathing. And how do they keep you alive? They put you on a ventilator. So of things otherwise being equal in that you're healthy, most of us would consider this to be an ordinary obligation to restore ourselves, be cured of this illness and go on living a healthy and productive life after that.

But consider the case of someone who's had cancer of the esophagus that was repaired by surgery where they pulled some of the stomach up to replace part of the food pipe that was cancerous. Then the cancer recurred and chemo and radiation were used and the patient did pretty well for a while. Then the cancer recurred again and the patient was brought into the emergency room with a fistula between the food pipe and the windpipe, with pneumonia, and stomach juices going into his lungs. Under those circumstances, we could put the patient on a ventilator. It could keep him alive a few days, or a few weeks, but it would only prolong the inevitable. The patient, otherwise in pain, could not be cured, and under those circumstances, it would be reasonable for any human being who is a good steward of his body, recognizing both his dignity and his finitude to say, this is enough. "I don't have to do this; the burdens are disproportionate to the benefits for me in these the circumstances." The same technology, the ventilator, was ordinary in one circumstance and extraordinary in the other. So you can't say ahead of time whether a treatment is ordinary or extraordinary.

Take another example, antibiotics. One might say, "Antibiotics are always ordinary, aren't they?" No. It depends on the circumstances. If any of you were to get pneumonia right now and I would give you pills for five days and cure you, and then you told me that the burden of that was disproportionate to the benefits, I would say, in the style of Joan Rivers, "can we talk?" I would think something was wrong there. But take the same patient who had pneumonia because the stomach juices were going into his lungs. Could that patient judge that even though the antibiotics might keep him alive a little bit longer, that the burden of being stuck with the needle and the cost to other people using these expensive antibiotics would make it disproportionate to the benefits? Yes. So, antibiotics in that circumstance could be an extraordinary or morally optional means of care.

It's not how many bells and whistles something has. It's not in the abstract whether this technology is ordinary or extraordinary. It's always the application of the technology to a particular case. And the adjective, extraordinary, is something that modifies your obligation, not the technology. It's not that the ventilator is extraordinary; it's your obligation to use it that is extraordinary. Because it's easy to confuse ordinary and extraordinary and there are common language uses for those two words, some people like to use proportionate vs. disproportionate. I prefer ordinary or extraordinary because it has a richer sense of the tradition.

On the basis of our current discussion, what is the worst thing that you could write in a living will? "No extraordinary means!" Because we don't know what it means until we know about you in a particular setting. It's too vague. When would you withhold or withdraw life-sustaining treatments? Either when it's biomedically limited, when the treatment won't work, which is basically a medical decision, or when the burdens outweigh the benefits which is typically a decision that our tradition says is made by the patient. Before Immanuel Kant applied the word "autonomy," patients were deciding in our tradition they could refuse the doctor's orders for treatment because in their judgment the burdens outweighed the benefits. And even when we're deciding for other people the perspective we ought to take is that of the patient. It's not about our obligation to care for the patient; it's about the patient's obligation to be a good steward of his or her life and to continue with these treatments. The perspective has always been that of the patient.

So what may be withheld or withdrawn? It's not just CPR. There are all kinds of other treatments that can be either not initiated or discontinued. We talked about ventilators, dialysis. A patient who's had two limbs amputated, two strokes, a heart attack and is blind from diabetes can say at some point, I don't have to go in the van three days a week to continue to be dialyzed. With St. Paul "I have fought the fight, I have run the race, I have kept the faith, and it's enough for me. I can go to God." You don't have to go into the Intensive Care Unit if you go into shock while you're in the hospital. You can decide to keep yourself out of the IC unit. We talked about antibiotics. If somebody's dying of liver disease and they're not making clotting factors and not a transplant candidate, they don't have to be transfused five times a week in order to keep going; they can refuse that. They can also refuse artificial hydration and nutrition. It's within the tradition. We'll talk a little bit about some nuances made from recent Vatican pronouncements. The tradition continues to encompass every kind of medical intervention.

Are withholding and withdrawing morally different? Sometimes people get worried about that. From a philosophical point of view, there is no difference. If you have grounds for not starting a treatment then you have the same grounds for stopping the treatment if you have already started it. There shouldn't be any difference between the two. For most religions, that's the case. There's no difference between not starting and stopping the treatment.

There are some exceptions, such as in Orthodox Judaism, with respect to ventilators because they are considered a continuous treatment as opposed to a discrete treatment, e.g. dialysis. Here is a quick case of a classical Jewish solution to the question of stopping a treatment once it's begun. There is actually now a law in Israel, developed with input from Rabbis, that you can put the ventilators on Shabbat clocks, or timers that are used to turn on the lights for Shabbat. So when Mrs. Schwartz's ventilator goes off at 8 a.m., you can make a decision whether to restart it even though you couldn't stop it. That's pretty clever Jewish reasoning.

There are some fundamentalist Christians who also believe that you can't stop the ventilator or some other treatments once you start them. But that is not the case for Catholic Christianity. We have never made a distinction between withholding and withdrawing life sustaining treatments. In fact, there may be good reasons to give it a trial. We think it may work out and start the ventilator and later, if it doesn't work, we can always make a decision to reassess and to stop it when things become clearer.

But when I talk to people – and if you are talking to any of your brothers and sisters about these time limited trials – recognize that it's psychologically harder on people to make the decision to stop it once started. Even though you could say theologically and philosophically there is no difference between withholding or withdrawing, it always seems like we are more involved once a treatment has started. Even though you are just as responsible morally for standing there and not starting it, when we turn the switch, it makes us feel a little bit more involved. So I counsel people that if you're going to do this, to think about that ahead of time, too, as one of the burdens in the decision-making. Can I actually stop it when I give one of these time-limited trials? But again, in the Catholic tradition there's no difference between withholding and withdrawing life sustaining treatments.

We haven't mentioned palliative care explicitly yet. I want to give quite a few cheers for the importance of hospice and palliative care. When we are talking about end of life care it does not just concern what we are *not* doing for the patient but all that we *can* do from the medical perspective for the patients who are dying. We can treat all of their symptoms better than we have ever been able to do in the history of humankind. We have many more kinds of treatments available for what I call neurocognitive symptoms, whether that's delirium or confusion, and we can treat them sometimes with drugs. If they are having seizures, we can treat those. Nausea can be treated pretty effectively now. Shortness of breath can be treated with just a little bit of morphine with doses that are lower than necessary to treat pain.

We can treat clinical depression in people who are dying. Depression is not natural when people are dying. It's natural to be sad but not to be depressed. We can treat people and treat those symptoms as well. But we also want to be sure that we look to give social and spiritual support for what I call agent narrative occasions of suffering, existential suffering. For instance, the sisters were talking about having their own sisters minister spiritually and humanly and socially in the nursing home as part of that support group for their sisters who are patients. Palliative care and hospice are expert at doing this. They did it as a grassroots movement, at least in hospice, when doctors weren't paying any attention. Nurses and medical lay people just decided that, "enough is enough; we'll take this into our own hands," and created the hospice movement in this country. It took medicine about forty years to catch up, but we now have palliative care as a medical subspecialty in the U.S.

We have to be very careful about how we treat patients and to make sure that we're treating them properly from a medical point of view. The cartoon says, "Before we try assisted suicide, Mrs. Ross, let's give the aspirin a chance."

"Before we try assisted suicide, Mrs. Ross, let's give the aspirin a chance."

Mae West's version of the rule of double effect:

"Whenever I face one of those difficult choices between two evils, I always pick the one I haven't tried yet"

I used to just have the quote without the picture of Mae West but most of my medical students don't know who Mae West was. Here's the real rule of double effect. An action is not intrinsically wrong in itself if it has two effects. Even if you foresee the bad effect, as long as you only intend the good effect, then the bad is not the cause of the good effect. If you have a proportionate reason for acting – the good outweighs the bad – in that situation you can go ahead and do it. Let me walk you through an example, in the case of morphine, so that you understand it very clearly. Then I'll give you an example that doesn't work so that you really understand it. So is the use of morphine indicated in a case? We know that drug has multiple effects. What are some of the good effects of morphine? Relieving pain, relieving shortness of breath. What are some of the bad effects that morphine might have? Respiratory depression – slowing people's breathing – is one effect and can, in fact, accelerate their dying. If you give the drug rapidly, it can drop people's blood pressure.

There are people who worry about addiction, nausea or other potential side effects. But the people we're most concerned about say, "Oh, you're Catholic. You're against euthanasia and assisted suicide. How can you give people morphine if you know that potentially it is going to shorten their lives by decreasing their breathing rate?" Is it intrinsically wrong to give people morphine? No. Otherwise, we would not do it after surgery like we do all the time. – In fact, if I end up on a deserted island, give me the newest antibiotic "du jour" and morphine and I'll be able to do most of my medicines for myself. But as someone who's morally opposed to euthanasia, I do give morphine to a patient who's dying. I'm giving it for pain relief. It may, at the same time, shorten that person's life by decreasing the breathing rate.

Let's take the example of the patient with the esophageal cancer that I talked about. If I'm giving this patient morphine because he's in severe pain from this acid burning in his lungs, I'm foreseeing the possibility that I might decrease his respiratory drive. But, is that my aim? No. My aim is to decrease and relieve his pain. Is it necessary for morphine to stop somebody from breathing in order for morphine to work? No, of course not. Then, we would never use it if everybody stopped breathing. So the bad that we're worried about is not the cause of the good. It even works in different receptors within the brain and the nervous system. In fact, the dose that is usually necessary to relieve pain is typically much less than the dose that would be necessary to stop somebody from breathing. If any of you have treated a heroin addict – heroin is related to morphine – there are people who use lethal doses practically every single day and still keep surviving. So the bad is not the cause of the good effect. And in the case of that patient who is otherwise dying of esophageal cancer with its latest complications, would my obligation – recognizing that I must comfort patients always – to relieve his pain not outweigh the bad effects of potentially shortening his life? Yes. So under the rule of double effect we can do that.

Now, one caveat is that in most cases people who resist the use of morphine do so probably because the respiratory depressant effects of morphine have been exaggerated. It's actually a very safe drug. We talked about the heroin addicts who come close to killing themselves. Here's another example, just to make the point. Derek Humphry, founder of the Hemlock Society wrote his book, *Final Exit*, a few years ago. It's basically a how-to book on suicide, from the Hemlock Society. The whole book is written in large print so you can read it if you have cataracts. But in really bold print it says, "Don't try to store up morphine or other drugs like that in order to try to kill yourself, because you're likely to fail."[3] It's really a much safer drug than most people think so that the errors that are typically made are to underdose pa-

---

[3] Derek Humphry, *Final Exit: The Practicalities of Self-Deliverance and Assisted Suicide for the Dying* (Oregon: Hemlock, 2002).

tients rather than overdose. So you give patients enough medicine to relieve their pain. That's what you're aiming for and the likelihood that you're going to hasten their death by doing that is pretty low.

One more example that I'll give to make sure that you really understand comes from Court TV. I don't usually watch this show but I did when Jack Kevorkian was on trial. His lawyer, Geoffrey Fieger, actually invoked the rule of double effect in defense of Dr. Kevorkian. He said, "My client, Dr. Kevorkian, when he was using carbon monoxide on people wasn't intending to kill them. He was only intending to relieve their pain following the tried and true rule of double effect recognized by medicine and even the Catholic Church." If you were on the jury, you wouldn't accept this. Let's say that you are using carbon monoxide. This one action has two effects; one is to relieve suffering and one is to kill the patient. Is it intrinsically wrong to give someone carbon monoxide? Yes. But let's grant them that, for the sake of argument. Is it conceivable that you would give somebody carbon monoxide saying, "Well, what I am really intending is to relieve your suffering, I am not intending to kill you." No. That would be really hard to do if you know what you're doing. But let's even grant them that. How does carbon monoxide relieve pain? By killing people. So the bad is the cause of the good in this case. It does not follow the rule of the double effect.

Let me talk a little bit about feeding tubes, which is very important for a lot of people in light of the Papal Allocution of 2004 and the Congregation for the Doctrine of the Faith Responsa to the inquiry from the United States Conference of Catholic Bishops in 2007. Here are some points which I think are reasonable for all of us. One is that the word vegetative is an unfortunate term. It has led some people to call human beings who are very sick *vegetables*, and I think that that is an affront to human dignity. When people are in a vegetative state, they are not vegetables, and if you are a good Aristotelian, you understand the difference but most people don't. Actually, in Australia they have a very reasonable term for it. They call it post-coma unresponsiveness; someone who is awakened from a coma only when they open their eyes but they are still totally unaware of their surroundings. That's what a persistent vegetative state is; it's the state after coma when your eyes are now open but you're still not responsive. And I would affirm, and I think that all of us would affirm that patients in vegetative state are created in the image and likeness of God and have human dignity. They have no less rights than other patients and we have had no development of doctrine regarding this. Feeding tubes still fit within the rubric of talking about ordinary and extraordinary means of care. It only applies, all of this discussion, in a direct sense, to conditions like persistent vegetative state. So be very clear that we're not talking about progressive lethal illnesses like Parkinson's disease, for instance, of which the last Pontiff died. At the end of his life Pope John Paul II was unable to swallow well. When he went into the Gemelli Hospital the second and last time, a feeding tube was placed through his nose into his stomach and he had it taken out before he died. So Pope John Paul II does not teach that everybody has to die with a feeding tube. If people are progressively dying from something, when they are in the end stages it doesn't matter whether you feed them or not, they are going to die. In fact, hydration can even make it worse when one is dying by making the work of breathing more difficult so it can be discontinued. So realize that these teachings apply only to this very small group of people in persistent vegetative state. They do not apply to those with cancer, or Lou Gehrig's disease, or Parkinson's disease, Alzheimer's disease, or any other disease where people are progressively dying from an underlying condition.

> In principle, there is an obligation to provide patients with food
> and water, including medically assisted nutrition and hydration
> for those who cannot take food orally.[4]

The words "in principle" have people confused but it means "as officially explained, the Catholic tradition." That means that it's ordinary unless it's overly burdensome. So even in these cases it can be overly costly. So the Congregation for the Doctrine of the Faith says that if you are over in Uganda and you are in persistent vegetative state, you probably won't survive to be declared in a persistent vegetative state to begin with. You have to spend about $1 million to get to the persistent vegetative state but it can be too costly in certain places to

---

[4] Ethical and Religious Directives for Catholic Health Care Facilities, n. 58 (revised, 2009).

keep people alive. It can be ineffective. Feeding tubes can be associated with complications, bleeding, infections or with physical suffering for the patient either from other diseases which they are suffering or from the feeding tube itself. Someone even in the persistent vegetative state could licitly, under current Catholic teaching, have the feeding tube removed.

Left uncommented on is whether you can ever forgo for other reasons such as for charity. Can you forgo it because you say in your advance directive that you don't want this money being spent for this purpose? The tradition encompasses an individual making those kinds of judgments. Or the traditional justification for the monk refusing the doctor's, and even the abbot's insistence that he undergo an amputation not because of the pain but because of the horror of living without a limb. It's a *vehemens horror*[5] in the tradition, so is it possible for someone to say that?

It's a great concern when others make that kind of judgment for a patient. But if someone makes that determination maybe it can be expressed in a living will. But here is what it says in the latest Ethical and Religious Directive, so it is very clear for everybody. "In principle" – which then implies the tradition for everyone – "there is an obligation to supply the patient with food and water including medically assisted nutrition and hydration for those who cannot take food or water orally. "We use feeding tubes all the time for people in the intensive care unit if they think that they will get out of it, if they have cancer and are undergoing chemotherapy, and this extends to patients in chronic and presumably irreversible conditions. But, "medically assisted nutrition and hydration become morally optional when they cannot reasonably be expected to prolong life or when they would be excessively burdensome for the patient by causing significant physical discomfort resulting from complications in the use of the means employed." This includes those in the end stage of any kind of chronic condition whether it be neurological, malignant, HIV infection, tuberculosis, or any other terminal condition. If a person is dying it's natural to want to stop eating at the end of life, they don't have to have feeding tubes put in.

"As a patient draws close to an inevitable death from an underlying progressive and fatal condition, certain measures to provide hydration

---

[5] *Vehemens horror*, an intense and overwhelming emotion of horror provoked by the use of those means.

and nutrition become excessively burdensome and therefore are not obligatory in light of their very limited ability to prolong life and provide comfort." And for 99% of people in end stages of progressively chronic diseases, this is the best thing to do.

Hospice nurses' wisdom says that it's better to die dry than to die wet because you can actually make things worse for a person by putting in an I.V. since their lungs can fill with fluid making it more difficult for them to breathe. This is the way we die; people stop eating when they die. It's natural and it's part of what we do and the Church is not insisting on anything different. Cardinal O'Connor did not have a feeding tube when he died of brain cancer. The pope did not have a feeding tube when he died of Parkinson's disease.

This is a fresco in Santa Croce in Florence, Italy. I think it's a portrait of death with dignity. I don't see any feeding tubes in this picture. I don't see a ventilator; I don't see an I.V. tube. I see a man surrounded by people who love him. Part of Francis's chronic condition at the end of his life was the excessive tearing. The General Minister and brothers made him go see the doctor in Rieti who cauterized his temples.

The treatment did not work. So what did the doctors suggest when the treatment did not work? Let's try it again. And what did Francis say? No! Basta, right? Enough! He refused the extraordinary means of care that were being offered to him. Things that he recognized that the doctors didn't, that might be more burdensome than beneficial for him. He, as you know, without a feeding tube had some morsels of almond cookies that Lady Jacoba brought him, he shared some bread with the friars and died surrounded by people who loved him, who cared for him, cared about him, prayed for him, prayed with him. You notice here that this friar is looking at the soul of Francis as it departs from his body. It's a really intimate portrait of death. It even has one of the friars kissing the stigmatized hand of Francis. That's death with dignity. If it was possible in the thirteenth century, isn't it possible in the twenty-first, particularly for Franciscans?

He Knew Long in Advance the Time of his Death: Ethical Issues in End-of-Life Planning

Thomas Nairn, O.F.M.

Do Franciscans die differently from other people? At first glance, this seems to be a meaningless question. Franciscans face the same end-of-life issues that others do. The ethical issues involved in end-of-life care decisions – and consequently in the planning for the end of life – are no different for members of the Franciscan family than for other people. Yet, the fact that we follow Francis of Assisi, someone who embraced death as a sister, should make a difference regarding how we plan for the end of life as Franciscans. In light of the Franciscan tradition regarding death and dying that I discussed earlier,[1] this essay will investigate the distinctiveness of that tradition by focusing on three areas of end-of-life planning: (1) general preparation for decisions at the end of life, (2) advance directives, and (3) the spiritual preparation for death and dying.

Preparing for End-of-Life Decisions

> These things St. Francis bore for almost two years with all patience and humility, giving thanks to God.... He committed his care to certain brothers who were deservedly dear to him.... These tried with all vigilance, with all zeal, with all their will to

---

[1] This essay is a companion piece to "'Fixed with Christ to the Cross': Dying in the Franciscan Tradition," found elsewhere in this volume and is dependent upon some of the material found in that essay.

foster the peace of mind of their blessed father, and they cared
for the infirmity of his body, shunning no distress, no labors,
that they might give themselves entirely to serving the saint
(1C 102).

Health care decision making in the U.S. is often an experience
that more reflects our nation's individualism than the communal nature of the Franciscan family. In fact as we look to the issue of preparing for the decisions that may be needed at the end of life today, we
almost immediately enter into a potential clash of values involved in
the choices that a sick member of the Franciscan family or her or his
surrogates must make. On the one hand our Catholic and Franciscan
vision speaks of the care that is owed a sick person who is seen as a
member of the community – as the story of St. Francis suggests. On
the other hand U.S. law strongly supports the value of autonomy and
the person's right to make his or her own decisions regarding end of
life care. Individual autonomy tends to trump all other concerns.

U.S. law understands the principle of autonomy in a very particular way. In 1891, the U.S. Supreme Court explained that:

No right is held more sacred, or is more carefully guarded, by
the common law, than the right of every individual to the pos-
session and control of his own person, free from all restraint
or interference of others, unless by clear and unquestionable
authority of law.[2]

This court opinion was based on an even earlier explanation articulated by Michigan Supreme Court Justice Thomas M. Cooley,
who described autonomy as "the right to be left alone."[3] At first glance
this emphasis on autonomy seems fitting for end-of-life decisions. It
acknowledges the appropriateness of such basic questions as: "What
kinds of treatments are acceptable or not acceptable to me? Where
and how do I want to spend my last days? Who will make end-of-life
decisions if I am prevented from making them?" Yet if one looks below

---

[2] Justice Horace Gray, Union Pacific R. Co. v. Botsford 141 U.S. 250 (1891).
[3] Thomas M. Cooley, *The Elements of Torts* (Chicago: Callaghan and Company,
1888), 29.

the surface of these questions, one realizes that the answers depend to a great extent upon the religious and moral values a person holds.

The exercise of autonomy is further complicated by contemporary medical technology. The very successes of technological development have helped to create a situation where most people expect that technological interventions are always necessary, will always be successful, and therefore should be demanded. Daniel Callahan has coined a term to describe this faith in technology, "technological monism":

> The use of technology is ordinarily the way in modern medicine that action is carried out: to give a pill, to cut out a cancerous tumor, or to use a machine to support respiration. With an ethos of technological monism, all meaningful actions ... are technological, whether technological acts or technological omissions. What nature does, its underlying natural causes and pathologies, becomes irrelevant. No death is "natural" any longer – the word becomes meaningless – no natural cause necessarily determinative, no pathology fatal unless failure to deploy a technology makes it so.[4]

Technological monism, this belief that all real actions in medicine are technological, can in turn lead to what Callahan calls "technological brinkmanship," which he describes as "pushing aggressive treatment as far as it can go in the hope that it can be stopped at just the right moment if it turns out to be futile."[5] In reality, however, such brinkmanship often does not succeed. Physicians pursue aggressive treatment for their patients beyond reasonable hope for success, because once they have begun a course of action, they do not know when or how to stop. It has been recently noted that "as death approaches, the first inclination of medical professionals is often to bring more options to the bedside – another intervention, a promising research protocol."[6] Medical technology, with its promise of health and human flourishing, when joined to the sheer number of options made available to dying patients or their surrogates, can become a threat to such flourishing.

---

[4] Daniel Callahan, *The Troubled Dream of Life: In Search of a Peaceful Death* (Washington, DC: Georgetown University Press, 1993), 68.

[5] Callahan, 192.

[6] Anne Drapkin Lyerly, et al., "Risk and the Pregnant Body," The Hastings Center Report 39, 6 (November-December, 2009): 35.

How can members of the Franciscan family respond? First of all, Franciscans do not understand freedom as the sheer number of options one has or simply the ability to choose one's preferences. Rather, we see freedom as arising from one's commitment to the good. It involves accepting that some options are indeed better than others and the acknowledgement of appropriate criteria to guide one's choices. This understanding of freedom requires that we understand not only what choices we have but also the reasons why we choose. In trying to understand these reasons, Ethical and Religious Directives for Catholic Health Care Services (ERDs)[7] can serve as a helpful guide. The ERDs were developed by the Catholic bishops as a compendium of Church teaching regarding the identity and integrity of Catholic health care.

The fifth section of the ERDS, dealing with care for the seriously ill and dying, states quite succinctly that: "The task of medicine is to care even when it cannot cure."[8] In Catholic thought, respect for the dignity of the person means that one truly care for the patient. In many cases, these converge. It does not necessarily mean that every choice a patient makes is proper. When patients are appropriately resisting the onslaught of disease, they should have their caregivers' support. True caregivers, however, will also be honest with patients and will acknowledge the time when aggressive treatment directed toward cure is no longer caring. Again, the ERDs explain:

> Life is a precious gift from God has profound implications for the question of stewardship over human life. We are not the owners of our lives and, hence, do not have absolute power over life. We have a duty to preserve our life and to use it for the glory of God, but the duty to preserve life is not absolute, for we may reject life-prolonging procedures that are insufficiently beneficial or excessively burdensome.[9]

Thus the Catholic understanding of life is that it is a precious reality and must be respected. Nevertheless, in an age of medical brink-

---

[7] United States Conference of Catholic Bishops, Ethical and Religious for Catholic Health Care Services, Fifth Edition (Washington DC: USCCB, 2010).

[8] Ethical and Religious Directives, "Introduction," Part V, 25/12. The ERDs are published in two formats: The first page number refers to the 4x9 inch version and the second to the 8½ x 11 inch version.

[9] Ethical and Religious Directives, 29.

manship, we need to reclaim our moral tradition of "ordinary" and "extraordinary" (or "proportionate" and "disproportionate") means.[10] The ERDs indicate how we might sensibly engage in such a task:

> Physicians and their patients must evaluate the use of the technology at their disposal. The use of life-sustaining technology is judged in light of the Christian meaning of life, suffering and death. Only in this way are two extremes avoided: on the one hand, an insistence on useless or burdensome technology even when a patient may legitimately wish to forego it and, on the other hand, the withdrawal of technology with the intention of causing death.[11]

It is important to note that the ERDs call upon us that we avoid two extremes, not only euthanasia but also what has come to be known as "medical vitalism," the insistence on useless or burdensome technology. It is only in terms of a middle ground that the Church's traditional teaching regarding the distinction between ordinary and extraordinary, or proportionate and disproportionate, means can be understandable today.

The teaching does not prescribe a hard and fast rule regarding specific medical procedures, but rather urges prudent decisions regarding the benefits and burdens of a particular medical treatment for a particular patient. This is part of the Catholic tradition's understanding of moral theology, which articulates that virtue is always in the middle and vice at either extreme. In emphasizing that we are not obliged to use extraordinary or disproportionate means, the tradition does not deny the good of technology or state that some lives are not worth living. Rather, it calls us to accept the fact that medical technology has limits.

In light of the above, Franciscans are able to speak – as others do – about the rights of the dying. Such rights have had a variety of articulations. An especially helpful list[12] has been developed by David Kessler, a writer on dying and grief and a colleague of Elisabeth Kübler-Ross:

---

[10] Congregation for the Doctrine of the Faith, "Declaration on Euthanasia," 1980.

[11] Ethical and Religious Directives, Introduction to Part Five.

[12] A subsequent printing of Kessler's work was titled "The Needs of the Dying." See note on page 46.

- The right to be treated as a living human being.
- The right to maintain a sense of hopefulness, however changing its focus may be.
- The right to be cared for by those who can maintain a sense of hopefulness, however changing this may be.
- The right to die in peace and dignity.
- The right to express feelings and emotions about death in one's own way.
- The right to participate in all decisions concerning one's care.
- The right to expect continuing medical care even though the goals may change from "cure" to "comfort" goals.
- The right to have all questions answered honestly and fully.
- The right to be free of physical pain.
- The right to be cared for by compassionate, sensitive, knowledgeable people who will attempt to understand one's needs.
- The right to express feelings and emotions about pain in one's own way.
- The right to seek spirituality.
- The right to express feelings and emotions about death in one's own way.
- The right to understand the process of death.
- The right not to die alone.
- The right of children to participate in death.
- The right to expect that the sanctity of the body will be respected after death.[13]

By acknowledging such rights, we Franciscans both show our respect for the dying sister or brother and witness to the fact that death itself is also a sister to us.

ADVANCE DIRECTIVES

So, when even against his will it was necessary to smear medical remedies on his body, which exceeded his strength, he spoke kindly one day with a brother whom he knew was ready

---

[13] See David Kessler, *The Rights of the Dying: A companion for Life's Final Moments* (New York: Harper Collins Publishers, 1997), especially ix.

to give him advice: "What do you think of this, dear son? My conscience often grumbles about the care of the body. It fears I am indulging it too much in this illness, that I am eager for fine lotions to help it. Actually none of this gives it any pleasure, since it is worn out by long sickness, and the urge for any savoring is gone."

The son replied attentively to his father, realizing that the words of his answer were given to him by the Lord. "Tell me, father, if you please, how attentively did your body obey your commands while it was able?" And he said: "I will bear witness to it, my son, for it was obedient in all things...." The brother said: "Well, then, my father, where is your generosity? Where is your piety and your great discernment? Is this a repayment worthy of faithful friends?

... Is it reasonable that you should desert a faithful friend, who risked himself and all that he had for you, even to the point of death? Far be it from you, father, you who are the help and support of the afflicted; far be it from you to sin against the Lord in such a way" (2C, 210-11).

In the United States there have been two basic kinds of advance directives, the living will and the durable power of attorney for health care, although the latter document has a variety of names. The idea of advance directives began to be developed in the United States in the 1960s, but it was not until 1976 that California became the first state in the nation to legally sanction living wills. Within a few years, most states had similar legislation.

The living will is a document used to help direct physicians dealing with end of life care in circumstances where patients can no longer speak for themselves. They normally contain very general language such as the following:

If at any time I should have an incurable and irreversible injury, disease, or illness judged to be a terminal condition by my attending physician who has personally examined me and has determined that my death is imminent except for death delaying procedures, I direct that such procedures which would only prolong the dying process be withheld or withdrawn, and that

I be permitted to die naturally with only the administration of medication, sustenance, or the performance of any medical procedure deemed necessary by my attending physician to provide me with comfort care.[14]

It has been precisely the general language of the document, however, that has made it less than helpful. Many physicians consider the language too ambiguous to guide them with end-of-life decisions that need to be made.

To deal with this difficulty, a second kind of document was developed, variously called a durable power of attorney for health care, a health care proxy, health care power of attorney, or something similar. Again California led the way in 1984 by legislating the nation's first law regarding the durable power of attorney for health care. This second sort of document is a written legal document that not only articulates a person's treatment choices but also designates a person, called an agent, who has the legal responsibility of communicating the person's treatment wishes when he or she becomes incapacitated. The principal may also limit the power of an agent by means of the document. In 1991 Congress enacted the "Patient Self-Determination Act" which stipulated that all hospitals receiving Medicaid or Medicare reimbursement must ask whether patients have or wish to have advance directives.

Even though advance directives were developed as a means of preserving patient autonomy, they can also be used by members of the Franciscan family as a way to express our values and to consult with others in making these important decisions. The ERDs state that "Each person may identify in advance a representative to make health care decisions as his or her surrogate" but adds that "decisions by the designated surrogate should be faithful to Catholic moral principles and to the person's intentions and values."[15] Preparing advance directives can become a time to discuss one's faith commitments, values, and consequent wishes with the trusted relative or friend who one has chosen to be one's agent.

During their short history, there has been some controversy surrounding these documents. Some fear that such documents can be-

---

[14] This excerpt has been taken from the statutory living will form from the state of Illinois. See Ill. Rev. Stat., Ch. 110 1/2, Para. 703.

[15] Ethical and Religious Directives, 25.

come part of the slippery slope toward euthanasia. In light of this, it is important to remember two things: (1) Our Catholic tradition has acknowledged the importance of these documents and the right and responsibility of Catholics in executing these documents. (2) These documents are tools that can be used either well or poorly. When executing such documents it is important to understand what one is doing. Especially for members of the Franciscan family, one of the most important aspects of the use of such documents is that it gives us permission to speak to our loved ones and others about the commitments and values that guide the decisions we make.

SPIRITUAL PREPARATION FOR DEATH

> With Christ as leader [Francis] resolved to do great deeds, and although his limbs were weakening, he hoped for victory over the enemy in a new struggle with a brave and burning spirit.... In that grave illness that ended all suffering, he threw himself in fervor of spirit totally naked on the naked ground, so that in that final hour, when the enemy could still rage, he might wrestle naked with the naked. Lying like this on the ground, stripped of his sackcloth garment, he lifted up his face to heaven in his accustomed way, and wholly intent upon that glory, he covered with his left hand the wound in his right side so that no one would see it. And he said to his brothers, "I have done what was mine; may Christ teach you yours" (LMj 14:1, 3).

St. Francis presented his particular vision of death and dying to people living in the early thirteenth century: "All praise be yours, my Lord, through Sister Death, from whose embrace no one living can escape!" (CtC, 12). By the fifteenth century this vision had already changed. The Black Death had devastated Europe. People lived under the continual threat of early or sudden death. Death, judgment and the possibility of eternal damnation was on everyone's mind, making dying itself something to be feared.[16] People went about their lives

---

[16] See my first essay in this volume, "'Fixed with Christ to the Cross': Dying in the Franciscan Tradition." Note the differences in the tone and language even between the writings of St. Bonaventure (†1274) and St. Bernardine of Siena (†1380). This trend continued during the course of the next century.

believing in the fragility of life itself and in the certainty of death and God's judgment.

One response to this religious understanding of death was the development of treatises on the "Art of Dying," or the ars moriendi. Among other items, these treatises listed five temptations that the dying person faced and suggested corresponding remedies:

- In response to the temptation against faith, the reaffirmation of faith;
- In response to the temptation to despair, hope for forgiveness;
- In response to the temptation to impatience, charity and patience;
- In response to the temptation to complacence, humility and one's recollection of sins; and
- In response to the temptation to attachment family or things, detachment.[17]

As we ask what a similar treatise on the art of dying and its accompanying spirituality might look like today for members of the Franciscan family, it is helpful to return to the Ethical and Religious Directives. The introduction to Part II of the document, entitled "The Pastoral and Spiritual Responsibility of Catholic Health Care," explains how end-of-life care cannot be limited to the physical but should also "embrace the physical, psychological, social, and spiritual dimensions of the human person."[18] The introduction goes on to explain that "without health of the spirit, high technology focused strictly on the body offers limited hope for healing the whole person."[19] Spiritual care during sickness and especially at the end of life can help a patient cope with feelings of powerlessness in suffering and can make it easier for the person to see meaning, and even redemption, in suffering.

At first glance, this spiritual preparation seems relatively straightforward. As the ERDs suggest, "the follower of Jesus faces illness and the consequences of the human condition aware that our Lord always

---

[17] For a more detailed explanation of the ars moriendi see the Encyclopedia of Dying http://www.deathreference.com/A-Bi/Ars-Moriendi.html.

[18] Ethical and Religious Directives, "Introduction, Part II," 11/6.

[19] Ethical and Religious Directives, "Introduction, Part II," 11/6. The bishops are quoting their 1980 pastoral letter, "Health and Health Care."

shows compassion toward the infirm."[20] Yet, even the term "patient" implies both suffering and being acted upon, ideas that are not at home in our American culture. As patients face the limiting circumstances that serious and terminal illnesses force us to confront, sometimes it is difficult even for Franciscans to find meaning. This meaning, however, can be found in the Gospel. We realize that suffering is an evil, but we are also called in faith to realize that it does not demean the preciousness of the gift of life given us by God or the dignity of God's image in the sick and suffering person. Even though it is often difficult, it is possible to find grace in suffering. In fact, following the examples of Francis and Clare, we often realize that grace finds us in our suffering.

All of this implies that Franciscan communities and homes are places of faithfulness and care for our sisters and brothers who are sick. If our sick sisters and brothers find themselves more dependent upon others than they have been at any other time in their adult lives, other members of the Franciscan family must be dependable. If Franciscans are to witness to death as a sister, then the Franciscan family must not abandon their sick sisters or brothers but – as the early brothers around Francis – continue to care for them. This can be especially difficult for those among us who like to "fix" things. Especially at the end of life for a sister or brother, the task is not to fix things but rather to remain present – and often powerless – with the one who is facing death.

---

[20] Ethical and Religious Directives, "Conclusion," 33/16.

Conclusion

Do Franciscans die differently from other people? Perhaps the best answer to this question is that, although Franciscans do not die differently, nevertheless our tradition has important resources that not only help us in our own preparing for the end of life but also enable us to witness to important Gospel values before others: In a world that often denies death, members of the Franciscan family are called upon witness to faith. In a world that often exaggerates autonomy, Franciscans are called upon to witness to trust. In a world that often needs to be in control, Franciscans are called upon to witness to their acceptance of the reality of sickness and dying. In engaging in this witness, we demonstrate that we are true daughters and sons of St. Francis, whose last words still echo in our ears: "I have done what is mine to do, may Christ teach you yours" (LMj 14, 3).

SIGNS OF FUTURE GLORY
ETHICAL ISSUES AFTER DEATH

DANIEL SULMASY, O.F.M., M.D., PH.D.

Ethical questions don't end when someone is actually dead so it may
be wise to cover some of these topics, both in ethics and in spirituality,
as well as bereavement before we move into the final session. Specifically I'm going to talk about two ways to determine that somebody is
dead. I'll also talk about organ donation, autopsy, death certificates,
donating one's body, disposal of remains and the spirituality of bereavement.

Basically the first thing that everyone should be aware of is that
there are now – from a medical viewpoint – two standards for determining that someone is dead. The standard way used for almost
everybody that you care for and about is a cardiopulmonary standard,
that is when somebody's heart stops and they stop breathing. The cardiopulmonary definition of death is the standard way used, going back
to Shakespeare and King Lear. Death used to be determined by putting a feather over a person's mouth to see if they still are breathing. If
someone stops breathing and the heart stops then we determine that
he's dead. Typically death is determined by a physician although it can
be delegated in certain states to nurses, or hospice workers, or nurse
practitioners. And this delegation is done by a physician.

There is some intentionality about this, too, which is really kind
of peculiar to the twenty-first century, since the cessation of heartbeat
and breathing is the indication for cardiopulmonary resuscitation. So,
to some extent, the determination of death is also the indication for
cardiopulmonary resuscitation. So there is some intentionality now involved in our determination of death that we are not going to attempt

to resuscitate the patient when their heart stops and they have stopped breathing.

But there is another way that you may have heard a little about so I want to address it. Brain death is a second way that someone is determined to be dead. Someone who is brain dead is characterized in this way: totally unresponsive and examined twice, twelve hours apart. Someone who has suffered hypoxic insults and stops breathing, and then, when found, is brought in and put on a ventilator may actually be brain dead because the only thing that's maintaining body functions are the machines. This determination is made by examination at baseline, and again twelve hours later.

Certain conditions must be met: the person's condition cannot be due to a drug overdose, barbiturates cannot be present in the system, hypothermia cannot be the cause because people can be revived if they have just been pulled out of water and are very cold. The neurological examination provides evidence that pupils don't react to light, that a cotton swab over the eyes does not cause blinking, and that other aspects about eye movement are dysfunctional. In addition the person does not breathe on his own. This last aspect is determined very technically by stopping the ventilator. The apnea test is done by giving people 100% oxygen. This way, if they are not brain dead, this doesn't harm them. Then the ventilator is turned off. If, after ten minutes they haven't taken spontaneous breaths or the carbon monoxide level has raised to a point where a normal person, whose brain is functioning well would have breathed, they have no respiratory drive whatsoever, this means that the entire brain is dead.

So it's different from somebody who has PVS – persistent vegetative state, otherwise referred to as post-coma unresponsiveness – which means that just the top part of the brain has gone although the bottom part is still working.

If someone is brain dead, the *entire* brain ceases to function. The top part doesn't work because they are unconscious but also these bottom parts don't work either—the mid brain and the cerebellum and the brain stem don't work, and that's what we are determining with all those neurological tests. It's not just that they are unconscious but the lower parts of the brain that keep the person breathing which are purely reflexive have also been destroyed by whatever that insult was.

The other kinds of tests you may have heard about are really optional. You don't have to do an EEG to determine that someone is brain dead. It's optional. If there are some questions about it you may want to do one or do a brain scan, but really once the clinical determination is done and repeated twelve hours later it can be determined that this person's brain has irreversibly ceased to function. So when this happens, if the whole brain ceases to function, and that person's whole physiological integrity has been disrupted, we consider that individual to be dead.

So the connections between the endocrine system—the glands that keep us going and the nervous system – have been severed. The blood pressure is unstable. Their pulse is unstable and their body temperature will fluctuate wildly. All the centers in the brain have ceased to function to keep these going. Someone who is truly brain dead, even with maximum support, will collapse within fourteen days. That's why in fact it is determined ethically and legally that these persons are dead. They have ceased to be an integrated whole organism. They have ceased to function. Legally and metaphysically, these persons are dead.

There are some religious exceptions to this definition of brain death. The religious exceptions are largely for Orthodox Jewish people who object to this determination of death. The definition of brain death, however, makes possible the donation of organs once someone is determined to be dead. For instance, you can be an organ donor even for unpaired organs that are still viable if you are considered intrinsically dead. Some people may worry about this, but in 2000 John Paul II said,

> it is helpful to recall that the death of the person is a single event, consisting in the total disintegration of that unitary and integrated whole that is the personal self. It results from the separation of the life-principle (or soul) from the corporal reality of the person.[1]

So he's describing the metaphysical condition for accepting brain death as the disruption of the integrity of the entire person.

---

[1] John Paul II, Address to the 18th International Congress of the Transplantation Society, August 29, 2000.

Here it can be said that the criteria adopted in more recent times for ascertaining the fact of death namely the complete and irreversible cessation of all brain activity, if rigorously applied, does not seem to conflict with the essential of elements of the sound anthropology.[2]

So no matter what you may have heard about pushback from certain extremely conservative groups, the Church accepts brain death and you have this statement from John Paul II, which has been reaffirmed by the Pontifical Academy in 2008. The Catholic Church does accept brain death as a valid definition of death. You can then, in fact, become somebody who is a candidate for the donation of unpaired organs like the liver, or the heart or the lungs, or often the heart and the lungs together if you are brain dead. You may be approached about this when you fill out your driver's license where you can say that you are willing to be an organ donor in the event that you ever become brain dead and this can be done.

Of course, you can be an organ donor before death, too. Maybe some of you have actually been organ donors such as giving a kidney to someone else. There are also some incredibly altruistic people who donate to strangers. But most people do this for family members within their genetic match. It's a tremendously altruistic gift to give an organ of yours. God has been abundantly generous to us in giving us more than we need, which is a very good Franciscan notion. Again the Catholic Church completely accepts the concept and practice of organ donations; the Catechism even says that organ donation after death is a noble and meritorious act and needs to be encouraged as an expression of generous solidarity. So those of you who are thinking about things to tell your proxies and filling out the advance directive may want to think about this as well.

The National Organ Transplant Act of 1984 prohibits the buying and selling of organs in this country and the church remains firmly committed to the idea of not commercializing organs. There are some utilitarians and economists, notably at the University of Chicago, who are pushing people to sell organs. I've had a lively debate with Richard Epstein at the law school who has argued that the great thing about markets is that if one loses one's health care insurance, selling a kidney

---

[2] John Paul II, Address to Transplantation Society, August 29, 2000.

may keep you alive. I view that as an insult to human dignity to consider part of ourselves property that can be sold. So far the law prohibits that in this country. But the need is great.

Here you can see that the number of donors and the number of transplants have been decreasing while the number of people who are waiting for organs has been increasing.

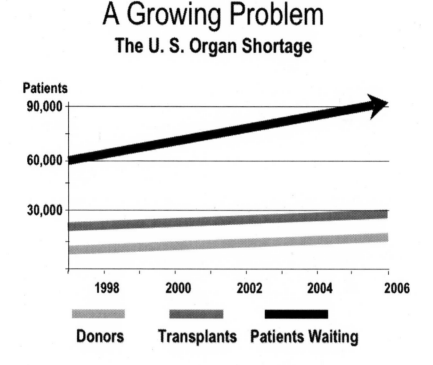

So, if people want to think about it as a way to be generous with your body after death, this is one thing to really consider.

A barrier to donation typically is the fear of being declared dead prematurely and the law has put procedures in place to prevent this. For instance, those who take the organs cannot be the same people who declare you to be dead. You need not be afraid then of not receiving optimal medical care. Again, for Catholics there is no moral problem for being an organ donor. In fact, it's actually encouraged.

You can donate either after brain death or after cardiac death. In the case of cardiac death, for example, let's say that you have been in a severe automobile accident. You're not brain dead but your family or the community has decided, on the basis of knowing you and what your wishes are, that they would stop life prolonging therapies. Under these circumstances, even if you are not brain dead you can become an organ donor.

In conditions such as these, for a person who has made the decision to refuse life support and also to be a donor, life support is considered an extraordinary means of care. Stopping life support would be done in a very controlled and programmed way. The ventilator is stopped, there is a wait of five minutes after the heart stops before the surgeon can come and take the organs. Five minutes has been determined to be the time limit after which someone's heart will not spontaneously restart. So after someone is declared dead under the cardiopulmonary definition of death, as long as people can ice down the body, and put cold fluids through, they can immediately remove the organs.

So you can be an organ donor for a paired organ – such as a kidney – when you are alive, or you can be an organ donor after you are declared to be brain dead or you can be a donor after cardiac death— three different ways to be an organ donor.

You should recognize that the body is property of the family and this goes back again to the Middle Ages. And even if you put it on your driver's license and advance directives, unless there is a state law that says that those trump the family, the family can then choose whether you are an organ donor or not. Some states are now allowing the driver's license and the advance directives to trump objections of the family. But most of the time you probably want both the family and the community to be in sync before somebody is an organ donor. Having that discussion ahead of time and having those directives would be most helpful in that way.

Another procedure that is sometimes necessary is that of the autopsy. Autopsies are permissible under Catholic teaching although there are some religions who object to it. Autopsies can be done for research, for teaching purposes, for improving the quality of care or for forensic purposes, if somebody died under suspicious circumstances. There are fewer and fewer of these being done and people object to them for strange reasons, e.g. not wanting to desecrate the body somehow, or thinking that there are religious objections. For Catholics, there are no religious prohibitions. The catechism states: "Autopsies can be morally permitted for legal inquest and scientific research."

Autopsies can be very valuable for people to learn from this. For instance, we heard about somebody being intubated incorrectly, how did that happen? For physicians to learn from all of their mistakes, autopsies are useful. Again the body is property. You cannot technically authorize your own autopsy. It must be done by the family or by the health care proxy. The health care proxy does, I should say, trump the family in terms of making that decision. These things can be done very quickly if you are worried about delaying a funeral. Autopsies are done very respectfully. The body can go to the funeral director quite promptly after the autopsy. Again, it's something that you can think about doing in the spirit of generosity towards future patients who might benefit from better physician care which can result from learning from autopsies.

Death certificates are public, legal documents in which the cause of death and contributing conditions are listed. They can be based upon the autopsy's result so if somebody has done an autopsy, typically it won't be filled out until the autopsy is being completed and again these are useful for epidemiologic purposes and for historical research. You should be aware that what goes on the death certificate is actually a public accessible document and you should all be aware of that.

The Code of Canon Law discusses disposal of your remains:

> The church earnestly recommends the pious custom of burying the body of the deceased to be observed; nevertheless, the church does not prohibit cremation unless it was chosen for reasons contrary to Christian doctrine.[3]

Many churches now have columbaria. I know that our Franciscan parish in Raleigh has a wonderful one. People who enter the church have to walk through a columbarium. So you see the community of the saints as you approach the church. And it does take up less room than the regular cemetery would.

We haven't really touched on bereavement that much yet. Bereavement is often neglected by the medical profession. We think our

---

[3] Code of Canon Law 1176 §3.

job is done once the person has died. It's ignored altogether in a lot of religious communities and really the connection with our brothers and sisters after death is not taken seriously. We sometimes think that it's only spouses and family that go through bereavement but we do grieve in deep ways and we need to be more conscious of that. We also need to be conscious of our own anticipatory grief. In many ways I think that lots of disputes that occur with family, for instance, about withholding or withdrawing life sustaining treatments, are really anticipatory grief. It's not an ethical issue about whether we want this person to stay alive or not; it's just the inability of letting go of somebody you love. And, it can happen to us too. We can be troubled by having somebody that we love and have lived with for fifty years die and we don't want to let go of them. We can put forth our objection to withdrawing life sustaining treatment as a substitute for the real issue which is anticipatory grief.

When this person is departing from us, we need to recognize that it's difficult. One theologian, Paul Ramsey, once wrote a really wonderful article entitled "The Indignity of Death with Dignity."[4] We forget that it's tough. I think Thomas Lynch is trying to help us understand that. It's tough for the person dying and it's tough for those remaining. We've got to come to terms with the reality of it. Karl Rahner,[5] in his wonderful little book on the theology of death says that death really is twofold—in its physical aspect our death is annihilation. At the same time it is the final affirmation of our genuine person, the sending over of one's personhood into the eternal mystery of God. Both are true at the same time. You can't emphasize one and neglect the other. Both are at the same time. So before death, it's wonderful to hear some of the rituals that are important for us, particularly as religious. This morning we talked about the wonderful idea of going back to the grave when the stone is laid, and the old Irish tradition of the Month's Mind Mass. These traditions, and many others, help us understand that the connection with the deceased has not ended. A wonderful thing happened to me as a novice when I went to the graveyard of St. Bonaventure's to begin my community experience with those who have gone ahead.

---

[4] Paul Ramsey, "The Indignity of 'Death with Dignity,'" *The Hastings Center Studies*, Vol. 2 No. 2 (May 1974), 47-62.

[5] Karl Rahner, *On the Theology of Death*, trans. Charles H. Henkey (New York: Herder and Herder, 1961).

And so I want to end with a little bit of meditation and I hope that it will be an introduction to our follow up. This, in case you don't recognize it, is actually part of the great mosaic at St. Francis Church, 31ˢᵗ Street in Manhattan. One of my lay friends, a guy that I went to high school with, once went to church there and said," Oh this is the Franciscan Sgt. Pepper Lonely Hearts Club Band." But it's the saints, right? It's the saints.

I want to talk a little about that as a transition into the end of our time together.

> And what the dead had no speech for when living, they can tell you being dead. The communication of the dead is tongued with fire beyond the language of the living.[6]

Those are the words from the poet, T.S. Eliot. And Eliot believes that we can actually pray to the dead. He believes that there's a communication between souls on both sides of the grave that is so profound that it cannot be captured with words. But what this could mean

---

[6] T.S. Eliot, "Little Gidding," in *Four Quartets* (Orlando: Houghton Mifflin Harcourt, 1968).

for those who have just lost a husband, or wife, or a child or a parent, or a very dear friend in the order is something we need to contemplate. Can one help a bereaved person to pray for the loved one he or she has lost? Can we talk to the dead, to our dead? I'm certain I can't answer all those questions for you this afternoon but I want to offer a few simple things that I think might be a gesture towards responses to some of them.

First, I want to suggest that praying to the dead has nothing to do with the world of the occult. I am continually frustrated by the popularity of TV shows that purport to contact the dead through various kinds of conjure. This sort of spectacle is both a physical exploitation of the dead and a manipulative exploitation of those who mourn them. We don't conjure the dead. And every honest superior should know that she will have no more control over a sister when she's dead than while the sister was with us. There's no conjury. Sorcery is not spirituality. Never attempt to manipulate God or manipulate those whose lives are now hidden with Christ in God.

Second, I do believe that the dead are with us in memory. However, if the dead only communicate with us through memory, then that communication really isn't genuine conversation. The memories we have of the dead are often beautiful and good. Memories come flooding into the lives of those who have recently lost loved ones as surging waves, at a moment's notice, sometimes without provocation. An old photo, a piece of jewelry can evoke all the meanings with which that item had been invested but which had never been noticed or verbalized in life. The smell of a closet can move one far beyond its confines. A few notes of a favorite melody can almost seem to bring the one we love before us humming. We connect these present events to past events, events warm in the memory that can bring a smile or a tear or both. But such experiences are not prayers to the dead. They are not in themselves instances in which one would really be talking to the dead or the dead would be talking to the living. Memories fade. It is a central Christian belief that people do not fade. We remember the names of only a very small number of extremely famous people who lived long ago—Moses, Plato, the Buddha, the apostles, Clare, Francis. Those whose fame lasts more than a few decades are but the tiniest fraction of 1% of all the persons who ever lived. It's always a challenge to name all the Franciscan saints. Few of us can even remember the maiden name of our great grandmother. One's own memory can't last more than a lifetime. Memories are good, but memories are not constitutive of true conversation with an immortal soul.

Third, some people are tempted to believe that the dead are remembered only through their deeds, through the fruit of the good works that one can attribute to them long after they're gone. For example, if somebody digs a water well, this might benefit thousands of people for hundreds of years. Or a woman might work extremely hard on a job outside the home saving enough to pay the tuition for a child whose career successes continue long after she's gone. Or one of our sisters or brothers might found some institution or orphanage or whatever it might be and it continues for generations. Those are good things for which we should be truly grateful to the dead. But you can't pray to a consequence and temporal consequences don't participate in any eternal transcendent reality. After all, eventually every garden that anybody ever planted will fade; eventually every well will run dry. No human deed is eternal. If I am present for those who follow me, my deeds will not be enough for them. The bereaved person cannot hope to pray to the abstraction of an ongoing set of good deeds from a loved one. That's not a conversation.

Yet, I do believe that there is a way in which the dead really are still with us and that we can pray to them and not just for them. This is not through the occult nor is it nearly an experience resident in memory, nor is it nearly a conscious recognition of their abstract presence to us as agents who offer good deeds that continue to bear fruit. I believe that the dead are really with us as persons. This is what we call, in Catholic theology, our faith in the communion of saints. Now one of my brother friars once told me a story about his conversation with a woman who had recently lost a very dear friend. And her friend had helped this woman and her family enormously after her husband had become quadriplegic in an accident. His assistance to this woman, to her husband, to her young son always with a good cheer had never faded over a decade. And he had become a part of the family. But her friend died suddenly and prematurely. And complicating her grief, a secret was exposed about her friend posthumously without his prior authorization and it was circulated widely. The woman became furious about this and inconsolably angry; not at those who had exposed the secret but at her recently deceased friend. She said, "I never knew this about him and suddenly I find out about it from other people. Why didn't he tell me? I am so angry. We were so close to him, like a brother, and a father and a son, all rolled into one. I'm so angry. Why didn't he tell me this when he was alive?"

Now this wise friar, in counseling her, saw that it would be no good to explain to her how this had happened or to inform her of the fact that many people keep a lot of things secret in life or suggest that her reaction might be a form of psychological projection. He's too smart for that. She was inconsolably angry and he knew that no rational arguments or insights could change her. And, so he said this, "Gosh, I don't know why he never told you, Catherine. Why don't you just go home and ask him? I'm sure that he can explain it to you better than I can." Immediately she began to weep. Why don't you just go home and ask him? That simple sentence expresses a profound belief in the communion of saints; a belief that the dead are still with us and we can commune with them. And "what the dead had no speech for when living, they can tell you being dead." That's the kind of real relationship with the dead and I believe it's possible.

But how is this so? Margaret Atwood in her poem "Variations on the Word Sleep" suggests ways that it might be so. She writes of a woman's feelings toward her husband. She doesn't set out in this poem to explain how the dead might be with us. But she explains how those we love remain with us. They're not just memories or abstract ongoing consequences. What she writes is this, "I would like to be the air that inhabits you for a moment only. I would like to be that unnoticed and that necessary."[7] All of those who have ever loved us inhabit us deeply right now. They are inside us, our brothers and sisters, like the air that we breathe, like the God to whom they have gone, the God that Augustine tells us is nearer to us than we are to ourselves. That's where the dead are with us. We may never have noticed but they have become necessary parts of who we are and they are really that close, close enough to talk to. They are part of what constitutes us now as persons. The people who have loved us deeply, even though they have died, have fallen into the mystery of God who is the love beyond all love and beyond all horizons and circumstances. This God, as Bonaventure once wrote, is the one whose center is everywhere and whose circum-

---

[7] Margaret Atwood, "Variations on the Word Sleep," in *Into the Garden: A Wedding Anthology* (New York: Harper Collins, 1993), 30-31.

ference is nowhere. The dead are with us in that holy love. That love is here in Denver and nowhere, in Chicago, in New York, in Rome and in Beijing—nowhere and everywhere. Gone and here. And if we who mourn would but listen, we could hear our dead tell us of that love. Love's language looms long beyond the lamentations of the living.

"Dying, as a Franciscan" Concluding Eucharistic Homily[1]

Michael F. Cusato, O.F.M.

Some of us, like myself, on this sacred but rough-and-tumble journey of life – often because of the driven pace of our lives – are harder than others on our feet. And those of us who have this difficulty know the comfort truly blessed that comes when someone pours soothing oil or cream, like a healing balm, over one's feet: slowly, patiently kneading that oil into our dry and damaged skin, deep down into those tired and aching muscles. Athletes, even more so, know this when their trainers massage those healing oils deep into those parts of the body that have been pulled and strained in the fray.

In ancient cultures, oil was prized and considered precious precisely because of its ability, when applied to the body, to restore vitality and strength to an individual. And, because of its restorative, revitalizing properties, that oil came to be considered a kind of conduit of divine power and energy and thus came to be used as the primary element in the ritual of the anointing of kings and queens. For it was the function – the duty – of the sovereign to provide his or her people the protection and strength and healing of the deity when in need. There is thus a connection between divine power, the medium of oil and a therapeutic healing action. It is for this that they had been anointed.

Our Scripture readings this evening are those of Sunday; but there are elements within them that can underscore some of the themes explored during our weekend. In the Gospel, we heard the famous confession of Peter in response to Jesus' query: "But you, who do you say

---

[1] Liturgical readings for the 12th Sunday of the Year are Zech 12:10-11; 13:1, Gal 3:26-29, Luke 9:18-24.

that I am?" And Peter's response was, of course: "You are the Christ of God!" That's a great translation! In other words: you are God's Christ; you are God's *Anointed*! Unfortunately, we sometimes miss the power of that term – *Christos* – as if "Christ" was the last name on the mailbox of "Joseph and Mary Christ"... But the name or title *Christos* means more than simply "You are God's *App*ointed!" To be the "*An*ointed of God" means that you are God's "chrism"; you are God's healing balm for all of us who are his people. Thus, it is a powerful description of Jesus' role in the world, on behalf of God, and for you and me!

And if Christ's role is to be a healing presence among us, so, too, is it the same role for those of us who bear the name of "Christian": we are to be, for each other, a "chrismatic" people: healing balm for one another, binding up the wounds inflicted by life during this sacred journey.

And do we ever need this balm for our journey! Because, as we are told further on in the Gospel: the road for the Christian will almost always, in some way, lead to the cross. Historically, of course, the cross began as a symbol of those evil forces in the world that conspired to definitively silence Jesus, whose bold message of love and justice and mercy threatened those supportive of, entrenched in, injustice. But over time, this same cross also came to embrace any and all forces we human beings contend with on a daily basis: the negative forces in human life – sickness and sadness, sin, reversal and failure, betrayal and hypocrisy, death. These are the daily forces that threaten to sap our energies and vitality and wear us down. And that is why we need from each other healing balm, the oil of gladness, the restorative touch of love and affection and care.

But: for Francis in particular, this cross – the cross of Jesus of Nazareth – was also the cross of Jesus *the Christ*: Jesus the Anointed One. It was the cross of the chrism of God: meant not only as a sign of wickedness and the destructive forces in human life but also – and especially – the symbol of healing for the human race. Salvation, yes, but not merely in the sense that one gains heaven. Rather the cross is the symbol of the possibility of transformed, healed human existence, made whole, transformed by grace – a grace made real and present through the restorative acts of our healing hands and hearts. We become the conduits of that healing grace.

In other words, the cross we are asked, each of us, to take up daily, has within it, commingled, not only the blood of human wounds streaming down the side of the cross from the hands and feet and side of Jesus, but also healing balm: the power of God released and sent forth in the resurrection and now made available to each one of us! The ridiculousness of the world, its folly and evil, are now commingled and offered to us but also overcome by the sublimity of God's life-giving restorative grace.

And so, just as we began this journey together this weekend, weaving together the strands of our own distinct journeys – male and female, sons and daughters of Francis and Clare and countless other saints of our family, so, too, now we will shortly attest in faith that, kneaded deep within our common journey, at its very heart, is the ever-abiding presence and healing power of the Risen Christ, who is balm for the life of us all. This is the *faith* and the *testimony* of those bold enough to put on the white garments of our baptism. But it is also our mission, as we go forth from here.

And that is why we can say with Peter to the One who has anointed us: "not only my feet, O Lord, but also my head and my hands and my heart as well!" (John 13:9).

NEW TITLES FROM
FRANCISCAN INSTITUTE PUBLICATIONS

COLETTE OF CORBIE (1381-1447) LEARNING AND HOLINESS
by Elisabeth Lopez and translated by Joanna Waller. In 1994, Elisabeth Lopez published, in French, a serious study of Colette and her reform movement. With a translation by Joanna Waller, this important work is appearing for the first time in English. 640 pages, Hardcover, Size: 6 x 9, ISBN: 1-57659-217-0, $50.00.

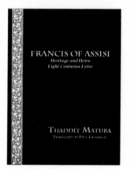

FRANCIS OF ASSISI:
HERITAGE AND HEIRS
EIGHT CENTURIES LATER
by Thaddée Matura, O.F.M. Translated by Paul Lachance, O.F.M. A fresh examination of how the Franciscan tradition has adapted and contemporized over 800 years. 112 pages, Tradepaper, Size: 6 x 9, ISBN: 1-57659-214-6, $25.00.

Special Offer – free shipping (up to $10) on either or both titles through June 30, 2011. Reference Special Offer NT2011.

FRANCISCAN INSTITUTE PUBLICATIONS
3261 WEST STATE STREET
ST. BONAVENTURE, NY 14778 USA
WWW.FRANCISCANPUBLICATIONS.COM
PHONE: 716-375-2062
FAX: 716-375-2113
E-MAIL: FIP@SBU.EDU

RECENT RELEASES

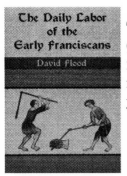

THE DAILY LABOR OF THE EARLY FRAN-CISCANS by David Flood, O.F.M., released 2010. Told from the vantage point of an historian, Flood leads the reader through his analysis of the early movement. 148 pages, ISBN: 1-57659-156-5, $30.00.

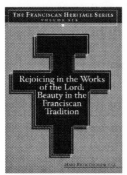

REJOICING IN THE WORKS OF THE LORD: BEAUTY IN THE FRANCISCAN TRADITION by Mary Beth Ingham, C.S.J. Released 2010. This volume focuses on the appreciation of beauty in the writings of Bonaventure of Bagnoregio and John Duns Scotus. 78 Pages, ISBN: 1-57659-205-7. $5.00.

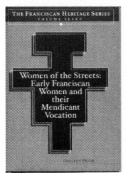

WOMEN OF THE STREETS, EARLY FRAN-CISCAN WOMEN AND THEIR MENDICANT VOCATION by Darleen Pryds. Released 2010. Rose of Viterbo, Angela of Foligno, Margaret of Cortona and Sancia, Queen of Naples pursued their religious vocation in the first century of the Franciscan Order. 84 pages, ISBN: 1-57659-206-5. $5.00.

Franciscan Institute Publications
www.franciscanpublications.com
Phone: 716-375-2062
Fax: 716-375-2113
E-mail: fip@sbu.edu

By Special Arrangement

The Early Franciscan Movement (1205-1239): History, Sources and Hermeneutics **by Michael F. Cusato, O.F.M. (2009).** This volume gathers together and updates previously published essays on topics related to the contested story of early Franciscan history (1205-1239), treating subjects such as the Franciscan approach to power and authority, the attitude of Francis towards Islam and the Crusades, the Privilege of Poverty, the connection between the two versions of the Epistola ad fideles, the relationship between the chartula and stigmata of Francis, the centrality of the Sacrum commercium, and the fall from grace of Elias of Cortona. By special arrangement with the Italian publisher, Centro Italiano di studi sull'Alto Medioevo (Spoleto).

$60.00

John Duns Scotus, Philosopher: Proceedings of "The Quadruple Congress" on John Duns Scotus (2010) Volume 1, edited by Mary Beth Ingham and Oleg Bychkov. From October 2007 through March 2009, four international conferences were held in honor of the 800th anniversary of the death of John Duns Scotus (d. 1308). This volume represents the papers from the first conference – held at The Franciscan Institute – which explored themes and issues from the *Opera Philosophica* of Scotus. Appearing in the prestigious series *Archa Verbi. Subsidia*, and co-published by Aschendorff (Münster) and Franciscan Institute Publications, these four volumes will represent the finest in contemporary scholarship on the Subtle Doctor today. $60.00

Coming Soon
from Franciscan Institute Publications

WORDS MADE FLESH: ESSAYS HONORING DR. FATHER KENAN B. OSBORNE, O.F.M. This volume contains papers by Bill Short, Allan Wolter, Zachary Hayes, Regis Duffy, Michael Guinan, Johannes Freyer, Antonie Vos, and Mary Beth Ingham, with topics ranging from Old Testament to Bonaventure, Duns Scotus, a work by Riccerio of Muccia, a Franciscan theology of the Word and the Franciscan tradition in the third millennium. Available May 2011.

COMMENTARY ON MARK, by Peter of John Olivi, translation by Robert Karris. Largely ignored until recently due to conflict with both Church and Order, Olivi may be considered one of the most original and interesting philosophers of the later Middle Ages. For most of his life (1248-1298) he taught at Franciscan houses of study in southern France and Florence, but is perhaps better known for his connection with the so-called "Spiritual" reform. Available May 2011.

INTRODUCTION TO EARLY FRANCISCAN SOURCES, VOLUME 1: THE WRITINGS OF FRANCIS AND CLARE OF ASSISI, edited by Michael W. Blastic, O.F.M., Jay Hammond, Ph.D., and J.A. Wayne Hellmann, O.F.M. Conv. This first volume presents the latest research by noted scholars and authors Luigi Pellegrini, Jean François Godet-Calogeras, Bill Short, Michael Blastic, Michael Cusato, Jay Hammond, Laurent Gallant, J.A. Wayne Hellmann, Ingrid Peterson and Lezlie Knox. Available May 2011.

Previous Titles in The Spirt & Life Series

Rule of the Friars Minor, 1209-2009: Historical Perspectives, Lived Realities (2010)   1-57659-212-X $20.00

Mirroring One Another, Reflecting the Divine: The Franciscan-Muslim Journey Into God (2009) 1-57659-157-3 $18.00

Daring to Embrace the Other: Franciscans and Muslims in Dialogue (2008) 1-57659-151-4 $18.00

"An Unencumbered Heart" A Tribute to Clare of Assisi 1253-2003 (2004) 1-57659-192-1 $14.00

Islam and Franciscanism: A Dialogue (2000)
1-57659-169-7 $10.00

True Followers of Justice: Identity, Insertion, and Itinerancy among the Early Franciscans (2000)
1-57659-171-9 $14.00

Franciscan Studies: The Difference Women are Making (1999)
1-57659-164-6 $12.00

Franciscan Leadership in Ministry: Foundations in History, Theology, and Spirituality (1997)
1-57659-132-8 $15.00

Refounding: A Franciscan Provincial Experiment (1994)
1-57659-037-2 $12.00

Mission in the Franciscan Tradition (1994)
1-57659-038-0 $15.00

The Care of Souls and the Rhetoric of Moral Theology in Bonaventure and Thomas (1993) 1-57659-034-8   **$10.00**

Ethical Method of John Duns Scotus (1992) 1-57659-03909   **$12.00**

The Franciscan Charism in Higher Education (1992)
1-57659-036-4 $12.00

Special Offer

Buy any two volumes in this series at regular price
and receive a third (of equal or lesser value) free.
Offer expires June 30, 2011. Use code: SL2011

Franciscan Institute Publications
www.franciscanpublications.com
Phone: 716-375-2062
Fax: 716-375-2113   E-mail: fip@sbu.edu